THE GREAT CROSS-COUNTRY RACE

or

The Hare and the Tortoise

An Entertainment for Children

by

ALAN BROADHURST

Proposed Production Plan

by IRENE COREY

ROYALTY NOTE

Cast

MR. FLEET	a Hare
MR. SETT	a Badger
MRS. WARREN	a Rabbit
MR. SPINEY	a Hedgehog
MR. PADDLE	a Water-Rat
MR. BRUSH	a Squirrel
MR. SLOE	a Tortoise
MRS. DARK	a Rook
MR. BASKET	a Dog
JACKIE	a very nice young human
ROBIN	another
A FISHERMAN	the common variety
MAUDE	one-half of a courting couple
GEORGE	the other half
MR. URBAN NOTCOUTH	a picnicker
MRS. URBAN NOTCOUTH	his wife
SOPHIA	his daughter
BRANDO	his son
FARMER BLACK	an irate farmer
MRS. STAINER	a near-sighted housewife

*Note: By doubling, the cast for this play can
be reduced to 7 men, 5 women.*

....

THE GREAT CROSS-COUNTRY RACE was first produced, under the title of "The Hare and the Tortoise," for a six-weeks run in January-February, 1965, by the College Repertory Players of Doncaster Technical College, in Doncaster, England.

Producer	Vivien Wood
Settings	Charles Pym
	Walter Monks
Choreography	Nellie Stagles
Costumes	Dorothy Wilson
	Joan Robinson

Principal Players:

Mr. Fleet	George Wann
Mr. Sloe	Maurice Horsfield
Mr. Basket	Gerald Coley

....

The Action of the Play takes place in and about the Woodlands. Yesterday—if it was fine; or, even this very afternoon.

Basic are permanent Wings and Sky Cloth.
The ground rows are changed each time, and a central Set Piece keys the Scene.

The Continuity Scenes take place on the Apron and in the Auditorium. The Action is continuous but the Intervals may be arranged as desired.

Scene 1	. . .	Frog Rock Quarry
Scene 2	. . .	The Bramble Thicket
Scene 3	. . .	The River Bank
Scene 4	. . .	The Grassy Bank
Scene 5	. . .	The River Bank Again
Scene 6	. . .	The Grassy Bank Again
Scene 7	. . .	Mr. Brush's Tree
Scene 8	. . .	The Cornfield
Scene 9	. . .	The Cottage Garden
Scene 10	. . .	Frog Rock Quarry

To My Grandson

MARK RODERICK

who happily timed his arrival to
coincide with that of Mr. Fleet
and Company: August 1964.

Scene 1—Frog Rock Quarry

A Ground-row of boulders.

Centre—Frog-shaped rock.

Downstage of the Rock is a smaller rock of a regular mound shape. It is, in fact, Mr. Sloe, the Tortoise, in retreat.

Around him, puzzled and arguing, are Mr. Sett, Mrs. Warren, Mr. Paddle, Mr. Spiney, and Mr. Brush. Mrs. Dark is a little apart, Up-left.

RABBIT. Well, I'm quite certain that it wasn't here yesterday.

HEDGEHOG. It must have been. Rocks don't grow in the night.

BADGER. But is it a rock? That's the point.

RAT. What else can it be?

SQUIRREL. It's hard like a rock.

RABBIT. It's rough like a rock.

HEDGEHOG. It's round like a rock.

BADGER. All the same, I've never seen a rock like it. And look at this sticking out—surely that is a leg?

HEDGEHOG. Whoever heard of a rock with a leg!

RABBIT. Well, there seems to be three more—one at each corner.

RAT. Please—you'll be saying that this stubby bit is a tail next!

SQUIRREL. And there's something here that could be a head—if it had ears—which it hasn't.

BADGER. A most odd rock.

HEDGEHOG. It would be an even odder animal.

SQUIRREL. Of course, there are some very odd animals. Far be it from me to be personal, Spiney, but you yourself—prickles instead of fur!

HEDGEHOG. At least I live on the ground and don't make my home in the trees like a skyflyer.

BADGER. Now, gentlemen, live and let live. We all have our little peculiarities.

RAT. Shall we get on with the sports? After all that's the purpose of this meeting.

BADGER. Quite. We were side-tracked by this—uh—thing here. I suppose it must be a rock.

9

(He sits on it).

It's as firm as a rock, anyway. Now, then—you've all sent in your suggestions for the events so we just have to see who's going to compete in what, and the Sports Day can begin. First, the Grass Eating Competition. Who's going in for that?

RABBIT. Me.

BADGER. Yes, Mrs. Warren, it was your suggestion. Now, who's for Grass Eating?

SQUIRREL. Not me, for one. Nuts, yes: grass, no.

RAT. Grass—ugh!

HEDGEHOG. We all know that Mrs. Warren could nibble more grass in an afternoon than the rest of us in a week.

BADGER. Mrs. Dark?

ROOK. Wha'?

BADGER. The Grass Eating Competition?

ROOK. It chokes my craw.

BADGER. Oh, dear. Well, no other entries. It looks as though you've won that, Mrs. Warren.

RABBIT. Oh, good. Is there a prize?

BADGER. We'll have to see. Next. Mr. Brush proposes a tree climbing race. Twice up and down the Leaning Pine.

RABBIT. I couldn't possibly. I even get dizzy on top of our bank.

RAT. Much too cold up there for any civilized animal. Swimming now—twice across the river. That's the thing. Four times—ten times—hundred times, if you like. I'll take all comers.

BADGER. We'll come to that Mr. Paddle—but let's settle the Tree Climbing entries first.

HEDGEHOG. No thank you.

BADGER. Mrs. Dark?

ROOK. Wha'?

BADGER. Tree Climbing?

ROOK. Climbing's for morons. I soar.

SQUIRREL. Well, really!

BADGER. Quite. How about the Swimming Race? Would anybody like to challenge Mr. Paddle?—No? Nobody. Oh dear.—Well here's one you can all join in. A most novel idea from Mr. Spiney —a Curling in a Ball and Rolling Down Hill Race.

10

Squirrel. Most undignified.

Rabbit. I haven't done it since my bunny days. I'm afraid I'm much too matronly now for that.

Rat. Who can curl in a ball on land? Animal Bob Apple in the water, if you like.

Badger. Oh, dear.—Mrs. Dark?

Rook. Wha'?

Badger. The Curling in a Ball and Rolling Down Hill Race?

Rook. Deplorable.

Badger. Then if nobody is going to enter these events, it just leaves the Cross Country Race. At least we have two competitors for that—Mr. Reynard and Mr. Fleet.

Squirrel. Reynard won't be entering, Mr. Sett. He asked me to say he was sorry but he sprained a paw yesterday on a hunt.

Badger. Not badly I trust!

Squirrel. Nothing, really. But he's resting up today. Apparently there's another hunt at the week-end which he doesn't want to miss. The Horses and Hounds do look forward to it so, and he hates to disappoint them.

Badger. What a kind fellow he is! Well, I'm sure we'll find plenty of others to give Mr. Fleet a run for his money.

Rabbit. Where is Mr. Fleet, anyway?

Rat. Late again—as usual.

Hedgehog. I've never known him be on time for an appointment yet.

Rat. He's certainly the dawdlingest animal.

Badger. Something will have delayed him.

Squirrel. Food, most probably.

Badger. Mrs. Dark?

Rook. Wha'?

Badger. Did you see Mr. Fleet on your way?

Rook. Snoring in the straw.

Badger. Sleeping again. It's too bad of him! Well, while we're waiting, who will enter for the Cross Country?

Hedgehog. Against Mr. Fleet! He's the fastest animal on earth.

Rabbit. I can do half a field quite quickly, but I'm afraid a Cross Country run would be far too much for me. I'd get dizzy.

SQUIRREL. Include a few trees as obstacles and I'd have a crack. But not Cross Country against a Hare. Oh, no!

BADGER. Mrs. Dark?

ROOK. Wha'?

BADGER. We must have somebody to race Mr. Fleet in the Cross Country.

ROOK. Circular tour?

BADGER. Yes. I've worked out an exciting course.

ROOK. All our family fly straight.

BADGER. This is most upsetting. We must have one race. How can we have a Sports Day if nobody competes against anybody!

ROOK. Warning! Warning!

(She hides in the wings. The others camouflage themselves to merge with the rocks, all curling motionless. Badger becomes an extension of Frog Rock.

The Dog bounds in.)

DOG. It's only me, Basket. Come on out.

(They uncurl. Rook re-enters).

BADGER. Why didn't you call?

DOG. Didn't want to make too much noise. *They* are with me. Or they think they are.

SQUIRREL. Slipped your lead again, eh?

DOG. No. We're hunting! What about that?

RABBIT. Hunting! Those two nice little doe humans? Oh, dear.

DOG. Not for you Woodlanders.

HEDGEHOG. Then what?

DOG. A new member of the family. Mr. Sloe. He got out of the garden.

BADGER. Mr. Sloe? What's his family name?

DOG. Tortoise.

BADGER. I don't think I know them.

DOG. This is the first one I've met. Came from a long way off, he says. What's a ship?

RAT. Like a floating log, I believe. But very big.

DOG. That's it then—he came from somewhere on a big floating log.

BADGER. What is he, a Woodlander?

Dog. I don't know exactly.

Rat. A Riverswimmer?

Dog. No. He'd sink for sure.

Hedgehog. A Skyflyer?

Dog. Impossible.

Badger. I suppose he is Animal?

Dog. Oh, yes—sort of.

Badger. Don't you know. How many legs?

Dog. Four—when you can see them.

Squirrel. Tail?

Dog. Sort of.

Squirrel. Head?

Dog. Sometimes.

Squirrel. Eyes?

Dog. I think so.

Rabbit. Ears?

Dog. Never saw any.

Hedgehog. What's his coat—fur or proper prickles?

Dog. Neither.

Badger. Then what? Feathers?

Dog. No. You won't believe this . . . Well, it seems to me to be rock.

Badger. Rock! — Stranger — dubious legs—no ears—rock? Oh my
goodness!

(He leaps up).

I do believe . . .

Dog. That's him. See what I mean?

Squirrel. But it's not alive is it?

Dog. Oh, yes. Sleeps a lot.

Hedgehog. But what's he doing here?

Dog. Just having a look round. Said he'd explored our garden and
wanted to meet you Woodlanders. My humans think he's run
away. Run away! That's good!

Rabbit. Why?

Dog. Because he moves so slowly that sometimes you think he's going backwards.

Badger. He seems to have reached here all right.

Dog. So he should have—he left last night.

Squirrel. Run away from the humans has he?

Dog. No more than me. But we both like a bit of intelligent conversation with friends. And poor old Mr. Sloe hasn't picked up any of the human language yet.

Rabbit. I'm sure I couldn't either. I do think you're clever, Mr. Basket—you understand every word they say.

Dog. True. The great thing, of course, is not to let on. Anyway today I'm with you. What's it to be?

Badger. It was to have been sports—but no one will compete. I wonder if your Mr. Sloe would enter? He can't run fast, you say, so the Cross Country's out, but he might—uh—Swim . . .?

(All are surveying the Tortoise: All shake heads on each query).

Climb the Tree . . .? Roll Down the Hill . . .? Ah! Grass Eating!

Dog. He eats grass and such. Day before yesterday he ate a whole dandelion leaf. Started at sun-up and took the last bit to bed with him.—Still, perhaps he's good at something.

(He raps smartly on the shell).

Anyone at home? Heh. Torto—wakey, wakey! It's me, Basket. I want to introduce you to my friends.

(Tortoise emerges and rises slowly to his hind legs).

Tortoise. Ah, it's you, Mr. Basket. Must have dropped off for a moment.

Dog. You found the Quarry, then.

Tortoise. Just as you directed. There was no one about, so I waited.

Dog. Good for you. Well, we're all here now. Let's see . . . This is Mr. Sett, Leader of the Woodlanders, Chairman of the Winter Stores Committee, Secretary of the Sports and Pastimes, and all that sort of thing.

Tortoise. How do you do, Mr. Sett.

Badger. Very pleased to make your acquaintance, Mr. Sloe. You've been puzzling us a little. From over the Hill, are you?

Tortoise. And beyond. My native home is over the sea.

Badger. Sea?

Rat. Where all the rivers meet. Otter's been. Told me about it.

They say there are Woodlands on the other side, but you can't see them, it's so big.

TORTOISE. Oh, there are, believe me.

DOG. This is Mr. Paddle.

TORTOISE. Delighted.

RAT. A pleasure.

DOG. And Mrs. Warren.

RABBIT. I'm so glad you're not a rock.

TORTOISE. My house? Yes, it's meant to look like a rock. Stops being pestered.

RABBIT. Do you take it everywhere?

TORTOISE. I find it convenient. It saves going home every night.

SQUIRREL. Ah, you're a relative of the Snails, I take it.

DOG. This is Mr. Brush.

TORTOISE. Pleased to meet you. Very distant cousins, the Snails. Very distant indeed. They haven't our swiftness of movement, you know. Our nearest relatives are the Turtle family.

BADGER. The Turtles?

TORTOISE. You don't know them? Pity. Charming creatures. The Turtles, the Terrapins and the Tortoise—we're quite a clan over the sea.

BADGER. And it's very nice to meet you. Mrs. Dark . . .?

ROOK. Wha'?

BADGER. This is Mr. Sloe. He has come to live with Mr. Basket and the little female humans. Thought he'd visit us.

ROOK. What for?

TORTOISE. Just to be sociable. It's very pleasant in the garden, but lonely. One pines for a friendly chat now and then.

SQUIRREL. I thought the humans were forever talking to the Garden Animals.

TORTOISE. They do. They do. But it's such gobble-di-gook, it makes my head swim. So if you don't mind, I would like to join you here in the Woodlands from time to time.

BADGER. Delighted to have you just whenever.

SQUIRREL. By all means. You must visit my Tree one evening: we'll have a bit of a crack.

TORTOISE. Thank you. Thank you.

(There is a commotion at the rear of the auditorium. Mr. Fleet has arrived. He charges down an aisle, and on to the stage).

HARE. Right, everybody, I'm here! Sorry to be a little late: Was delayed. Important conference.

(He is with them).

Are we all met? The Sports can begin. I'm here.

(He sees Tortoise).

Ah, who—what—is this?

BADGER. A new friend. Mr. Sloe. Mr. Sloe, meet Mr. Fleet.

TORTOISE. How do you do, Mr. Fleet.

HARE. Howdo. You competing in the sports?

TORTOISE. I had not really thought about it.

HARE. Just as well. Not much of a runner, I should say.

TORTOISE. I get where I want to be, you know.

HARE. Ah, but when?

TORTOISE. Slow and steady wins the race, they say.

HARE. Do they? Well, take it from me, they're wrong. 'To the Swift, the Lettuce'—my old school motto.

TORTOISE. I dare say you are right, Mr. Fleet.

HARE. I'm always right. And what's this on your back?

BADGER. Please, Mr. Fleet!

HARE. He don't mind me asking. You don't mind me asking, do you Mr.—uh . . .

TORTOISE. Sloe.

HARE. Slow. I should have remembered that easily enough.

TORTOISE. It is my back.

HARE. This great lump of whatever it is!

SQUIRREL. Shell. You know, Fleet—like Snails, only bigger. Terrapins and Turtles—same idea. Carry your house with you.

HARE. What's the point of that? He'd never get anywhere in a month of Sundays.

TORTOISE. You'd be surprised, Mr. Fleet, how we Tortoise do get around.

HARE. But not in athletic sports. I suppose we could use you as a finishing post.

(He turns away, rudely).

Why don't we start? I'll just win this race, then run over to
Hambledon Hill for tea with the Moles—it's only ten miles.
Where's Reynard?

SQUIRREL. Not coming. Laid up with a sprained paw.

HARE. That's what he says. Afraid of me beating him, more like it.

BADGER. I'm sure it's not that. Mr. Reynard is a very fine Cross
Country runner.

HARE. Horse radish! I can beat Reynard with one paw strapped
to my back! I can run faster and straighter and longer than any
animal in the Woodlands. I can run so fast, that if I set out now
to the Cabbage Field to fetch a head for dinner, I should meet
myself coming back!

HDGEHOG. If you didn't stop for a nap on the way.

HARE. What's that! I could stop for fifty naps, and still beat any of
you slow-coaches. And if you don't believe me, just enter for
the Cross Country now. Come on—anybody.

RABBIT. You know we wouldn't stand a chance against you.

HARE. I tell you what, I'll give any of you five minutes start. What
about it, Basket?

DOG. How d'you expect me to race you if my Greyhound cousins
can't catch you? I'm not built for speed.

HARE. No good asking you, Paddle—you'd trip over your own tail.

RAT. I'll swim you a mile up the river.

HARE. Fiddle-di-de—swimming! I'm talking about real animal sport
—running. And none of you are any good. Brush—he can't run
for nuts. Nobody can beat me.

BADGER. That's the last event gone west. It is a shame. I've been to
no end of trouble to arrange the course.

TORTOISE. Is it a long course, Mr. Sett?

BADGER. Three miles exactly. It starts here and goes to the Bramble
Thicket, then to . . . Wait, I'll show you. Mr. Spiney and Mr.
Brush, would you fetch the old gate I was working on, please?

*(Hedgehog and Squirrel exit, to return with a solid gate on which
is chalked a pictorial diagram of the Course).*

HARE. Thinking of issuing a challenge, Mr. Sloe?

TORTOISE. Just interested. We often had Cross Country runs at home.
Most enjoyable.

HARE. What did you use for legs!

TORTOISE. These I have served quite well.

(On comes the gate).

Ah.

Badger (*Lecturing*). Now, here's the Start—Frog Rock. First check point—the Bramble Thicket. Then to the River Bank: From there to the Grassy Bank; then to Mr. Brush's Tree; half a mile to the Cornfield; then past the end of the Keeper's Cottage, and a straight run home to here again in the Old Quarry and Frog Rock, where the runners have to pass Frog Rock and do one more full lap of the Quarry to win—There will be judges at each point, and Mr. Basket will take short cuts and be general referee.

Tortoise. Very, very interesting.

Hare. Too easy. Hardly worth running.

Tortoise. Very similar to our courses at home. Not too short and not too long.

Hare. Well, you're wrong again, fat legs. This race is too short *and* too long for any animal—except me. And to me it doesn't matter. Short or long—Hares can't go wrong. We Hares are the fastest runners on earth.

Tortoise. Mr. Sett . . .

Hare. We Hares are the most athletic creatures in creation.

Tortoise. Mr. Sett, I think I will . . .

Hare. We Hares have the longest legs and longest ears of all animals.

Tortoise. I think I will, if it's all the same to everybody . . .

Hare. We Hares are invincible—and bright and intelligent—and pretty—and witty—and charming—and no animal dares compete against us.

Tortoise. I think I will enter for the Cross Country Race.

Hare. We Hares in general, and myself in particular—What!

Badger. Are you sure, Mr. Sloe?

Tortoise. Yes, I would enjoy a good run.

Hare. You! You want to race me?

Tortoise. If you'd be so kind.

Hare. Ridiculous! I'd be past the winning post before you'd started.

Tortoise. In that case, you would be the winner.

Hare. Winner? Of course I'd be the winner! No—I won't do it.

Tortoise. Then I would be the winner. Mr. Fleet beaten at last.

Squirrel. That would be a tid-bit of news throughout the Woodlands.

Hare. But I can't be beaten if I don't run.

Hedgehog. And you can't win if you don't run.

Squirrel. Mr. Fleet refuses a challenge from a stranger!

Hare. I don't refuse a challenge. I just refuse to run against a fat-legged, hump-backed, earless old slow coach. I would be the laughing stock of the corn stukes!

Dog. You will be if my friend has a walk-over.

Hare. Walk-over! Crawl-over, you mean!

Rabbit. And he might win if you give him a good enough start.

Hare. Talk sense. He couldn't beat me if I gave him a half-way round start.

Tortoise. Oh, I don't want a start.

Hare. You seriously think you can run faster than me?

Tortoise. No.

Hare. Ah!

Tortoise. But I'm sure I can win the Cross Country Race. In fact, I think any animal here could beat you, young Hare.

Hare. What!

Tortoise. And, if I may say so, I think that some animal should have done it long ago.

Hare. Why, you . . .

Tortoise. Because, I'm afraid you really need a lesson. You strike me as being just a little too proud of yourself—too boastful—not to say, cocky, young Hare.

Hare. Will you stop calling me 'young Hare'! I am three! And in the prime of my animalhood.

Tortoise. Are you? I am twenty-four.

(A general gasp).

And am still a comparatively young tortoise. Now, do we race, or are you too scatter-brained even to start?

Hare *(Thumping his feet on the ground in temper)*. That does it! We race!

Rook. Warning! Warning! Withdraw! Withdraw!

(The Animals freeze as previously, albeit with heads cocked until the last second. The Hare merely leans nonchalantly against a wing, confident that, if he is spotted, he can run from danger. The Dog listens and sniffs.

We hear human voices—but NOT intelligible speech. We are with the animals and can understand their speech: We cannot, therefore, reasonably expect to comprehend human speech as well. Only Dogs and some of the Birds are so bi-lingual. But we can

*sense general meanings from the expression of the human speech
. . . and it is the general sense of what the humans say that is
indicated in our play. The articulations with which they express
it are as incomprehensible in detail to us as they are to our
animal friends.*

*So: two young female voices approach, making calling sounds.
Jackie and Robin are seeking Basket . . . It might be written:
"Ah-skit! Ah-skit! Oo-ah-oo? Skit—good og. Ear oy! Whistle.
O air iz at aughty og! Ah-skit! Ood og. Whistle. Ear oy!" Etc.
This applies to all human speech tonight, and Producers and
Artistes will no doubt devise their own expressive—and amusing
—gobble-di-gook. Certainly no more will be phonetically illus-
trated).*

DOG. It's all right. It's only my humans. Keep still. They won't see
you.

HARE. Let 'em. They can't catch me.

RABBIT. Are you sure they won't, Mr. Basket?

DOG. I don't know how the humans manage—they have ears and
noses and eyes, but they can't hear or smell or see. Not what we'd
call hearing, smelling and seeing. You stay put: they'll walk
all round, and not know you're here. Just hark at them!

BADGER. What are they saying?

DOG. They are calling me.

SQUIRREL. Oughtn't you to go?

DOG. Not yet. They don't really expect me to. Hear that? 'Good
dog.' Good dog!—It's funny: the more naughty a dog is, the
more the humans call 'Good dog.' Keep down now. I'll lead them
off. Back in a minute.

(He shouts—the Girls would say he was barking—off).

Here I am! Here I am! Just try to catch me!

JACKIE'S VOICE *(Is saying that she has heard Basket. Come on).*

ROBIN'S VOICE *(Is saying that he is a good dog and must come to them).*

(They run on. Two very pleasant young ladies in jeans).

DOG. Hello, you two. Nice to see you. Follow me. This way.

(He exits and re-enters, inviting).

JACKIE *(Is pleased to find him).*

ROBIN *(Wonders what he wants).*

JACKIE *(Thinks he wants them to follow).*

ROBIN *(Is sure he's found Tortoise: clever dog).*

Dog. Come on, my pretties, I'll soon lose you for a while.—Back in a minute, Mr. Badger—Come on, then.

(He exits with the Girls following. The Animals unfreeze).

Badger. Remarkable. I must say you garden dwellers seem to have the best of both worlds, Mr. Sloe.

Tortoise. It is a comfortable life—with kindly humans—I agree.

Rabbit. How Mr. Basket can understand them, I don't know!

Hedgehog. It's all very well not being seen, but one of them nearly stepped on me.

Hare. I don't know why you bother to hide. I never care if humans do see me—I can always run away. They run like beetles.

Squirrel. I don't mind if I'm in my tree. They've no idea of climbing.

Rat. Or swimming.

Rook. Or soaring.

Badger. They can't do anything properly, and yet they rule the world. Remarkable!

(Dog re-enters).

Dog. Soon fixed that. Poor dears, they're properly lost now.

Tortoise. Will they be all right?

Dog. Oh, yes—I'll pick them up later, and take them home.

Hare. Then we can start this Cross Country Race.

Squirrel. At last.

Badger. Mr. Fleet: Mr. Sloe—are you quite clear? The first Point is the Bramble Thicket. Mr. Slither will be there to see you through and put you on the way to the next place. Now, line up please. The Start is here.

(Tortoise commences his very slow walk to the line. Hare runs through a series of limbering-up exercises and physical jerks. Then a couple of sprint dashes across and back. He jogs loosely to the line—and Tortoise arrives at the same time, having travelled all of three or four yards).

Hare. Some race! Go ahead, start it. I'll go when I'm ready.

Rabbit. Please, Mr. Fleet. I always think the 'Ready, Steady Go' is the most exciting part.

Hedgehog. You must start together.

Hare. Oh, all right. It's a farce, though.

Dog. The humans say 'On your marks' now.

BADGER. That's what I'm going to say: 'On your marks,' then, 'Ready. steady—Go!'—'On your marks!'

(Hare immediately snaps down into a thoroughly professional sprint-start crouch. Tortoise does the same in double slow motion. Hare watches him: the others are embarrassed).

Ready!

(Hare comes up: Tortoise too, but incredibly slowly).

Steady!—Go!

(To a cheer, Hare shoots off . . . A few high stepping paces, then he marks time, and turns to watch Tortoise who hasn't made any perceptible movement.—Check: he has now: one foot is just passing the other . . .

From this moment until the end of the Race he never stops, but for two notable exceptions, but he is excruciatingly slow.

Hare stops jog-trotting on the spot, and wanders back).

HARE. You all right, old Tortoise? Rheumatics? Twinges? Can I get you a couple of crutches?—You won't mind if I don't wait at the finish to see you arrive, will you? My Dam said I always had to be in bed by mid-night.

(Tortoise passes him and exits, to appear sometime later in the auditorium, an extension of our Quarry, where he progresses— if that is not too dynamic a word for it—up an aisle).

Well, I hope you're all satisfied. Cross Country Race, indeed! It's bad enough beating Foxy Reynard and the like, but at least they finish on the same day that they start!

HEDGEHOG. You won't beat him standing here.

SQUIRREL. He's just pacing himself. You see, he'll come strong at the end.

DOG. It's all right. Mr. Fleet's just giving him that start he promised.

HARE. Did I say 'half way'? I could let him sight the winning-post and still catch him.

(He lies down. Tortoise reaches the auditorium).

RABBIT. There he is! Run, Mr. Sloe! Go on, run! Give him a cheer. Go on, Mr. Sloe—go on!

SQUIRREL. Run up, old fellow!

HEDGEHOG. You're doing fine!

DOG. Thunder on, Torto! Keep it up!

He stamps twice and they sing:

> Thunder on, Old Torto, thunder on
> Thunder on, Old Torto, thunder on
> For we want you to be there
> At the post before the Hare,
> So, thunder on, Old Torto, thunder on.

Rook. Encore! Encore!

Hare. Idiots!

Badger. Oh, dearie me! Oh. I forgot!

Dog. What's that?

Badger. I meant to tell him—tell all the competitors. At the Grassy Bank, I've had the Shrews put an arrow to point the way. It's just near your place, Mr. Spiney, but you might not be there in time. They have to follow the arrow up the side of the hedge, otherwise they'll go straight on and go miles out of the way. Mr. Sloe! Mr. Sloe!

(They all call).

Rabbit. He can't hear.

Hare. No wonder—he's got no ears!

Badger. But we must tell him. Mr. Sloe!—Oh, Mrs. Dark?

Rook. Wha'?

Badger. Could you fly over and catch him and tell him . . .

Hare. Now, don't panic, Mr. Sett. Calm down. I'll tell him.

Badger. Would you really, Mr. Fleet! That's very kind of you. At the Grassy Bank there's an arrow which . . .

Hare. I know. I know.

(He dashes off, to re-appear immediately in the auditorium and, in no time flat, catches up with Tortoise within yards of an Exit Door. Tortoise keeps moving).

Message from the Officials. At the Grassy Bank look out for an arrow. Very important. Miss it and you'll go wrong. Got it?

Tortoise. Yes, indeed, Mr. Fleet. Yes, thank you very much.

Hare. Not at all. I was just passing.

(Tortoise exits. Hare runs back).

Dog. He's told him.

Badger. Good—Good Earthworks, he's coming back!

Squirrel. Keep going, Fleet!

Rabbit. Mr. Sloe's out of sight!

Hare *(Regaining the stage).* I told him. He says, 'thank you very much!'

Badger. But I didn't mean you to come back, Mr. Fleet.

Hare. I thought you'd like to know he understood.

Badger. Yes. Yes, thank you very much. But the Race has started.

Rabbit. Oh do hurry, Mr. Fleet!

Hare. You think I ought to start?

Rabbit. Yes, yes!

Hare. I'm hungry.

Rabbit. You can't be!

Hare. I can be. I always am.

Squirrel. Hardly the time for a meal, I would have thought.

Hedgehog. He's well on his way now.

Dog. I'm off to the Bramble Thicket. Mr. Sloe will be there any minute.

Hare. I'll be there first, never fear.

Badger. And you others should be getting to your positions. Mr. Paddle, the River Bank.

Rat. Right.

Badger. Mr. Brush—your Tree.

Squirrel. Roger.

Badger. Mr. Spiney—the Grassy Bank, and please make sure that they follow the arrow.

Hedgehog. I'll roll up in plenty of time. It's no distance across the Meadow.

Badger. Mrs. Warren—see them through the Cornfield, but stay near to the hedgerow. Some very peculiar Humans frequent the fields now-a-days.

Rabbit. I'll slip into Mrs. Burrow's place and watch from there.

Badger. Mrs. Dark?

Rook. Wha'?

Badger. You stay here with me. Perhaps you'd be good enough now and again to soar up and tell me if they are coming.

Rook. Pleasure.

Hare. So you're all leaving me. And nobody's anything to eat?

Rabbit. Not here, Mr. Fleet—but if you'd like to pop in after the Race, I've some lovely turnip-tops fresh nipped this morning.

Hare. Where there's a fill—Hare's away! See you later. Right, let's start the race.

Badger. I've already started it!

HARE. Just give me the 'Ready, Steady—Go' and I'll show you what a real start is.

BADGER. Oh, very well. It's all most peculiar. On your marks. Ready —Steady—Go!

(And Hare, indeed, goes like the wind: up the aisle, and out).

Well, that's that. Off you go.

SQUIRREL. I'll report back here as soon as they've passed me.

HEDGEHOG. And me.

RABBIT. If Mr. Sloe isn't too far behind, I should be able to scurry back for the Finish.

BADGER. See you all here about tea-time.

DOG. Yes. All except poor old Torto. If Fleet keeps that up, he'll pass him before the first check point. See you later.

(They have made their various exits. Badger settles against Frog Rock for a snooze).

BADGER. Well, what do you think of it, Mrs. Dark?

ROOK. Wha'?

BADGER. What do you think of our Race between a Hare and a Tortoise?

ROOK. Deplorable!

BADGER. Oh, I don't know. Mr. Sloe might win.

ROOK. Boars might soar!

BADGER. I expect you're right. Ah well, it's a pleasant afternoon.

(He nods off. Rook stands stonily).

Number One Tabs Close . . .

CONTINUITY SCENE ONE:

Jackie and Robin enter to Centre. They are looking for, and calling, Basket.

They hold a short conference, and arrange to circle in opposite directions.

All this, of course, in human gobble-di-gook.

Jackie exits right: Robin exits left.

Seconds later, Mr. Sloe starts his cross from right. He has travelled a yard, when Mr. Fleet dashes past him.

Mr. Fleet 'double-takes,' then circles him three times at speed and shoots off left, making motorbike noises.

Mr. Sloe has maintained his steady .001 m.p.h., and, eventually, he too exits left.

Number One Tabs open on Scene Two.

A Ground-Row of brambles. Centre—a large Bramble Bush.

Hare dashes on from right.

HARE.   I'm here! I'm first! Check me through, Mr. Slither.

(But the Grass Snake is not to be seen).

Mr. Slither? Where are you? Come on—can't stop: this is a race. Mr. Slither?

(He nips round the bush, poking his head into it to see; getting tangled and scratched).

Oo-ah. Mr. Slither! Where are you?—Oo, these brambles!

(He extricates one ear, badly snagged).

Well, if you're not . . .

(He hears Mr. Slither in the very centre: we don't).

Oh, there you are. Come on out, you're supposed to be an Official.

What?—Oh, are there?

(He listens).

You're right—there are humans about. Yes, you stay hidden. I'm off—Uh-uh!

(The voices of the girls have neared, calling to each other. Now they enter: Jackie Up-Right: Robin Up-Left.

Mr. Fleet is balked, and he squats Centre below the middle of the thicket, making himself very small).

JACKIE *(Asks if Robin has seen Basket).*

ROBIN *(Hasn't. Has Jackie?).*

JACKIE *(No. He is a naughty dog).*

ROBIN *(Agrees. She is going to give him a good spanking when they do find him—Oh, what lovely blackberries).*

JACKIE *(Oh-yes! She's going to have some).*

ROBIN *(As well).*

They come Centre Up-Stage of the Thicket: pick, exclaim and eat. They work round, coming nearer and nearer to Mr. Fleet. He peers this way and that: becomes increasingly worried, and, when the Girls are half-way round each side, starts—hurt as it does— to work his way into the middle of the bush.

The last we see is his agony-wracked face as his body is completely hidden, and the Girls join up Down-Centre.

(Mr. Basket is heard off-Left).

Dog. Mr. Slither! Anybody arrived yet? Have the runners passed you?

(He bounds on).

Whoops! My humans!

Jackie and Robin *(Are saying that Basket is there. He's a good dog: he's a bad dog. He's to come here at once, etc.).*

(There is much dodging as Basket evades them. What to the humans are playful yappings, are in fact messages to any animals in the vicinity—and, of course, us).

Dog. It's all right, Mr. Slither. I'll lead them off.

Hare. Do! Then come back and get me out of these thorns!

Dog. You in there, Fleet?—Oops! Missed me, duckie!—Don't go away.

Hare. How can I go away when I'm stuck!

Dog. Won't be long—Come on, my dears—chase me!

Hare. Be quick. That Torto-mi-jig will catch me up!

Dog. Don't fret. Here we go!

(A final dodge, and he runs off with the Girls in full cry after him. There are upheavals and strugglings in the centre of the bush, and we can—if we are just a bit malicious, and who of us isn't?—enjoy Mr. Fleet's predicament).

Hare. Humans! Always poking about in the Woodlands where they've no right to be—Owch!—It's all right for you, Mr. Slither, you snakes are little and thin, and haven't got long fur and ears. Oh, my beautiful fur: it's coming out in great tufts! Oh, my lovely ears: they'll be cut to pieces!

(Mr. Basket enters left).

Dog. Here we are then. Lost them again. Now, what's to do?

Hare. Get me out of this tangle, that's what's to do! Come on, hold back some of these briars.

Dog. Right-ho.

(He essays).

Ooch, my paw!

(He tries again, but is defeated by the thorns).

Hold on, Fleet. Oo-ah! Heh, I'm getting caught up myself!

Hare. Will you get me out! Ow!

Dog. I'm doing my best. These thorns hurt. Yip!

Hare. I'm supposed to be in a race. D'ah!

Dog. You'll beat him easily. A-a-ah!

Hare. Not if I'm stuck in here. Gee-hup!

Dog. Well, you shouldn't have gone in. Yi-yi-yi!

Hare. I had to to escape from your humans. O-oo!

Dog. They wouldn't have hurt you—Ah-no! It's no good, Fleet. I'm getting scratched to pieces. You'll have to get yourself out.

(He sits biting thorns out of his person).

Hare. It's your fault, you get me out. Ee-ooo!

(Tortoise enters Down Right at the same sub-steady-pace).

Dog. Here's Mr. Sloe, now.

Hare. He can get me out. The thorns can't hurt him.

Tortoise. Hello, Mr. Basket. Check me through.

Dog. Stop a minute, Torto. Mr. Fleet's stuck in the brambles.

Tortoise. Mustn't stop. It's a race. The only way to win races—or anything else—is to keep at it.

Hare. But I'm stuck! Help!

Dog. If you could just make a hole in the bush. Wouldn't delay you very long.

Tortoise. I have to keep going, Mr. Basket. I can't make up time like other creatures.

Dog. But Mr. Fleet will die in there. This is an emergency.

Hare. Please, Mr. Sloe. Nobody can get me out but you. Unless a male human comes along—and then I should be for the cooking pot!

Dog. To oblige me, Mr. Sloe.

(Tortoise now left of Centre, circles to come below the bush).

Tortoise. If it is really a matter of life and death, then of course I will help if I can.

Dog. Good for you. Can you force a tunnel through to him?

Hare. Just stamp on the brambles. Hurry!

Tortoise. Very well.

(He opens up a hole with his fore feet and one hind foot, to the encouragement of the other two. Mr. Fleet attempts to come out but is still held).

Hare. It's not big enough. I'm still caught up!

Dog. Could you crash in backwards, Torto, and crush them down?

TORTOISE. That might do it. But if I get on my back, I cannot get up again. I'll manage this way. If at first you don't succeed, try, try again.

HARE. Do be quick, you silly old faggot! You're slower than a month of Sundays.

DOG. That's a fine way to talk to some-one who is doing his best to help you!

TORTOISE *(Amiably)*. Slow but sure. Slow but sure, I hope, young Hare. Here we go.

(He tramples well into the bush. With much scrambling and help from Basket, Mr. Fleet crawls out).

HARE. I've done it!

DOG. That's it, then, now the race can go on.

HARE. I'm off!

DOG. Just a moment—you ought to let Mr. Sloe have a start.

HARE. He refused a start.

DOG. Yes—but now, if he hadn't stopped to help you, he would have been well away.

HARE. He should have thought of that! His trouble is, that he thinks about as slowly as he runs.

DOG. But it's not fair!

HARE. All's Hare in love and war! Ta-ta. I'll tell them he'll be late! *(He runs off, Down-left).*

DOG. Of all the ungrateful selfish cheats!

TORTOISE. He's only young, Mr. Basket.

DOG. I'll 'young' him!

TORTOISE. Don't worry. The Race isn't over yet.

DOG. You did him a great kindness. He should reward you!

TORTOISE. If we only do kindnesses in hope of reward, they are no longer kindnesses—I'll just keep going. A lot can happen between here and the Winning Post.

(He exits Down-left).

DOG. I hope you do win, Mr. Sloe. I'll take the short cut to the River Bank. See you there.

(He runs off Up-left).

Number One Tabs Close.

CONTINUITY SCENE TWO:

Mr. Fleet enters from a rear auditorium door.

He makes his way down, unhurried but vigorous: jogging, doing training exercises, shadow-boxing and pausing to declaim at intervals . . .

HARE.   I am the fastest runner on earth! I am also very beautiful . . . No animal can beat me. I can out-run and out-smart the lot of them . . .

I wish one of them had even half my prowess. It gets boring winning so easily all the time . . .

I can lick them all . . .

I can see further: hear further: and run further than the rest of them put together . . .

And I am pretty, too . . .

(And if he gets any understandable back-chat from his audience, he must ad-lib further conceits to full bent, stopping short only of promoting a full-scale riot.

Number One Tabs open on Scene 3).

And here we are, Check Point Two—first, as usual.

Scene 3. The River Bank

A Bank Ground-Row.

*A Fisherman, surrounded by paraphernalia and creature com-
forts, including a full picnic spread, is reclining asleep in his little
canvas chair. His rod is propped, and the line dangles into the
river.*

*Mr. Fleet makes his way on to the set with some caution, but soon
realizes that this human is sound asleep.*

Hare.   Ah, a male human. The one that's always wetting worms.

(Mr. Paddle's head appears above the bank).

Rat.   P-sst!—P-sst!

Hare.   I wondered where you were, Paddle.

Rat.   He's been here all afternoon, the nuisance. It's all right to pass
through if you go softly.

Hare.   No hurry. Old Fat-legs is miles behind.

Rat.   You'd better not stop though. He might catch you up.

Hare.   Let him. I can run rings round him. —What have we here?

(He investigates the picnic boxes).

Hello, hello—I do believe . . . Yes, lettuce sandwiches! And fresh
tomatoes! Oh, very good! And what's this?

(Salad cream).

Milk?

(He sits).

Rat.   No. They put it on their greens. It's pretty awful stuff—not
fit for animals.

Hare.   Have you tried it?

Rat.   Once. One of them left a container lying around, and I had a
lick. Made me quite ill.

Hare *(Sampling)*. Oh, I don't know. Rather pleasant. Of course,
you lower River Swimmers haven't the cultivated tastes of we
Hares.

Rat.   It won't do you any good.

Hare.   Fiddle! If it's good enough for humans, it's good enough for me.

*(He liberally smothers the sandwiches with salad cream—and
salt—and pepper, and eats greedily).*

Rat.   What about the Race?

Hare.   What race?—Ah delicious! I always knew we Hares should eat something better than rabbit food—I can win that walking backwards . . . And special water in a container!

(Pop—which fizzes hugely when he un-stoppers it).

Oops!—Oh, very palatable!

RAT. I don't think that that is good for animals, either.

HARE. Not for you lower orders, certainly.

(Mr. Basket enters Right).

DOG. You're here, are you?

RAT. Not too loud—it's asleep.

DOG. Oh, him! What's his idea, wetting worms all the time?

RAT. He thinks the Under Water Swimmers will eat the worms and get caught.

DOG. Ridiculous!—Heh, Fleet, you ought not to hang around if you want to win.

HARE. Is Fat-legs still plodding on?

DOG. Yes. And he can't be far behind.

HARE. Plenty of time when he catches up. I'd give you one of these, but I'm afraid they're too delicious to waste on you.

DOG. Thank you very much!

RAT. He'll be ill.

HARE. Dry up, wet-head!

(He finds an apple—creams, salts and peppers it: then gobbles up).

RAT. Not that I mind his helping himself to the male human's food. Serve him right.

DOG. He's not doing any harm.

RAT. He would if I didn't stop him.

DOG. Stop him what?

RAT. Catching the Under Water Swimmers.

DOG. You mean to say that they really eat the worms?

RAT. Oh, yes. Especially the Tiddlers. You can't tell them. I spend half my day unhooking them, then tying on weeds, or sticking the hook under stones.

DOG. To stop him coming back?

RAT. Yes. But he doesn't seem to care. Comes back just the same. But I've a special surprise for him to-day.

DOG. What's that?

(Tortoise has entered the auditorium, and is coming down an aisle).

RAT.   Here he is! Here's Mr. Sloe!

DOG.   Come on. Torto—run up!

RAT *(To Hare)*.   You'd better be on your way.

HARE.   I'll just finish this.

(A huge slice of cake which he also salad-creams, salts and peppers. He washes it down with the last of the Pop).

DOG.   Come on! You've caught him up!

RAT.   He's going to pass you here!

DOG.   Thunder on, Torto!

RAT.   Mr. Fleet, you must run now.

HARE.   If you think so. But there's really no need.

(He rises—and is suddenly gripped by a tummy pain).

I can't.

RAT.   Can't what?

HARE.   Run. Oh, my stomach!

DOG.   Come on, Torto! Come on!

RAT.   Run, Mr. Fleet—run!

HARE.   I don't feel very well!

RAT.   I told you not to be greedy.

DOG.   You've got him, Torto!

HARE.   I'm dying!

RAT.   No you're not. It's only tummy-ache with over-stuffing yourself. It'll work off. Run.

(Hare staggers a few paces, and stops again. Tortoise reaches the set, from right).

HARE.   We ought to call a rest for a few minutes. All competitors.

(He rolls in agony).

RAT.   Mr. Sloe, will you agree to a rest for a few minutes?

TORTOISE.   Sorry, Mr. Paddle, must keep going. Check me through, please.

RAT.   But Mr. Fleet—has a bad stitch.

HARE.   It's not a stitch—it's my appendix! We Hares have more miles of appendix than any . . . O-oo! I'm dying!

Dog. Hard luck! On you go, Torto.

Tortoise. I expect he'll get over it.

Dog. See you at the Grassy Bank. Don't forget to look for the arrow.

Tortoise. I won't.

(He exits, Down-left).

Rat. Get up, Mr. Fleet. Keep moving and it'll wear off.

(He helps Hare move around).

If you'd kept running properly as I told you, this would never have happened.

Hare. I was hungry.

Dog. You have to eat after races; not while they are on.

Rat. That's better. Is it going?

Hare. A bit.

Rat. Fine thing if Mr. Sloe beats our champion! You'll never live it down.

Hare. I'll beat him. I can catch him and pass him, even if I am critically ill. We Hares are the bravest . . .

Rat. Never mind all that now—just get after him.

Hare. You watch me. I can beat him on two paws.

(He staggers off holding his tummy).

Dog. He's the boastingest animal in the Woodlands.

Rat. He can be very aggravating at times.

Dog. My little female humans' female parent says that 'Pride comes before a Fall' whenever they start swanking.

Rat. Well, he certainly swanks, does Mr. Fleet.

Dog. And if he doesn't beat Torto, he'll surely fall. Come on, let's cut across to the Grassy Bank.

Rat. You go on, Mr. Basket, I've a little job to do here.

Dog. With the male human?

Rat *(Tapping his nose significantly).* I'll cure him for good of wetting worms near my place—I'll see you at the finish.

Dog. Right—Oh, keep out of sight for a moment. My little female humans will be passing. Mustn't lose them altogether.

Rat. I'll pop in the river 'til they've gone.

(He nips over the bank, then his head re-appears. Dog calls right).

Dog. Heh, you two! Hello! I'm here—can you hear me? Come on.

(We hear the Girls distantly: their indefatigable calls and whistles. They approach. Dog exits Up-left. They run on, and check at the Fisherman).

JACKIE *(Wonders whether or not to ask him if he's seen a dog).*

ROBIN *(Thinks he looks as though he's been asleep a long time. He might be angry).*

DOG *(Off).* Come on! Come on! This way. Find me!

JACKIE *(He's over there!).*

ROBIN *(Yes. Come on!).*

They call and whistle as they run off.

Rat shakes his head, amused. He comes to the Fisherman's side and cautiously hauls—not reels—in the line as . . .

Number One Tabs close.

CONTINUITY SCENE THREE:

Tortoise enters the auditorium, and ploughs on steadily.

As he is nearing the Pass Door (or steps) to the stage, Hare reels in. To great groanings and puffings, he struggles on at nothing like his best pace but, even so, much faster than Tortoise.

Tortoise achieves the stage.

Hare passes him Down-Centre: his look of malicious triumph somewhat marred by grimaces of pain.

He may not be the most lovable of Hares—but at least he's game.

He exits Down-Right.

Tortoise, unmoved, follows to exit some long seconds later.

Number One Tabs open on Scene 4.

Centre—a Grassy Bank.

Stuck on the top is a crude stick arrow pointing Left.

Waiting and enjoying the afternoon sun, is Hedgehog.

Groans presage the entrance Down-Right of Hare.

HEDGEHOG. Somebody coming!—This way: here's the arrow.—You, Mr. Fleet. Well, I'm not surprised, I must confess.

HARE. Oo-oh!

HEDGEHOG. What's the matter?

HARE. I've been poisoned!

HEDGEHOG. Poisoned!

HARE. That rat Paddle. Made me eat some human-type food.

HEDGEHOG. But why?

HARE. How should I know why! Doesn't want me to win, I suppose.

HEDGEHOG. This is dreadful! It's your tummy?

HARE. Tummy, and all over.

HEDGEHOG. Could you manage a raw egg?

HARE. Would it help?

HEDGEHOG. Very good for settling an upset tummy. Not only that, all the best runners suck raw eggs.

HARE. Is that a fact!

HEDGEHOG. Oh yes. Makes them go like the wind.

HARE. Does it?

HEDGEHOG. Most assuredly. Luckily, I have one. Found it by the hay-stack, freshly laid this morning. Very hard to come by these days with all the hens living in blocks of flats. Years since I found a full clutch of eggs in the open.

HARE. I'll try anything once.

HEDGEHOG. Better come to my house. You are all right for time, I expect. Mr. Sloe will be miles behind.

HARE. He's not! I've only just managed to pass him.

HEDGEHOG. I am surprised! How does that come about?

HARE. First he pushed me in the Bramble Thicket, then he wouldn't agree to a halt when I was nearly dying.

HEDGEHOG. Most unsporting. Well, come on quickly and have this raw egg, and you'll be as right as rain and twice as fast. Oh—do you suck or dip?

HARE. Do I what?

HEDGEHOG. Suck the egg through a hole, or break it and dip your paw in it and lick it? I suck myself.

HARE. How do I know? I've never had a raw egg.

HEDGEHOG. A treat in store. You'd be a dipper, I should think. You haven't got a sucking face.

HARE. It's a very pretty face, let me tell you!

HEDGEHOG. Oh, yes, yes, quite. Nothing personal. But I'm sure you're a dipper. I'll open it for you. Come on.

(He leads off Up-Left. Hare sees the arrow, has a thought, and calls . . .).

HARE. Ow-ch! Be with you in a minute, H. H. Got a thorn in my paw.

HEDGEHOG *(Off)*. You are in the wars.

HARE *(Lifting the arrow and reversing it)*. And that will do more than slow old Fat-legs down—it'll send him backwards!

(He dusts his paws, and treats us to a few well-chosen, self-laudatory observations).

Not only are we Hares gay, open and frank—we are extremely cunning! . . . If you can't beat 'em—cheat 'em! There are two sorts of animals in the Woodlands: the Hares and the Squares . . . You may have noticed that besides being fantastically fast and incredibly clever, I am also preternaturally pretty! . . . We Hares . . .

HEDGEHOG *(Off)*. It's ready, Mr. Fleet. Come along.

HARE. Coming old friend.

(To us).

Sucker!—Coming, no great hurry

(To himself).

—now!

(He exits, Up-Left. Dog bounces on Up-Right calling).

DOG. Anybody about? It's me—Basket!

HEDGEHOG *(Off)*. I'm here, Mr. Basket.

(His head appears).

I'm just giving Mr. Fleet some nutricious raw egg.

DOG. Oh. Mr. Sloe gone through?

HEDGEHOG. Not yet.

(His head withdraws).

Come in for a bit. We will hear him.

Dog. Right.

(He 'takes' the arrow: weighs it up . . .).

Those dreamy Shrews! They can't see for looking! Give them the simplest job and they get it wrong! Good thing I spotted it— Mr. Sloe would be sent back!

(He turns the arrow to point in the original and correct—Left).

And that Hare can't afford to hang about if he wants to win. Where are you?

(He exits Up-Left.

Tortoise enters Down-Right. He has ample time to study the arrow as he approaches it . . .).

Tortoise. Mr. Spiney? Mr. Basket? I'm checking through.

Hedgehog *(Off).* It's Mr. Sloe!

(He enters).

Dog *(Off).* He's here! He's here!

(He enters).

Come on, Torto! Thunder on! Everything all right?

Tortoise. Doing very nicely, thank you. Have just got my second wind.

Hedgehog *(Calling).* He's here, Mr. Fleet! Hurry!

Hare *(Off).* Has he followed the arrow?

Hedgehog. Yes. He's on his way. You must get running again!

Dog. Go on, Torto—you've passed him again.

(Tortoise exits Down-Left).

Hare *(Off).* Don't fuss, H. H. It's a walk-over.

Hedgehog. But it won't be if you just sit there!

Hare. Coming.

(He enters quite slowly: yawns, stretches and goes through his limbering exercises).

Ah, I feel much better now. Very hospitable of you. Your only egg, too!

Hedgehog. That's quite all right—but do hurry.

Hare. Followed the arrow, did he?

Dog. Of course. Mr. Sloe may take his time, but he's not soft.

Hare. Oh, I agree. Hard as rocks, in fact. Especially his head!

HEDGEHOG. You really must try to catch him, Mr. Fleet. You'll be beaten!

HARE. First catch your Hare.

DOG. What?

HARE. Nothing. Family joke. Right, then—start me off.

DOG. You've already started.

HARE. Well, this is a fresh start. Just watch me fly. Hare to-day and gone to-morrow.

DOG. Mad as a May Queen!

HEDGEHOG. Do be quick!

HARE. So old Fat-legs followed the arrow, did he!

HEDGEHOG. Yes, yes! Hours ago!

HARE. Set me off then.

(*He studies the arrow, and takes up a sprint-crouch-facing the wrong way*).

DOG. You're facing the wrong—

HEDGEHOG. Onyourmarks—readysteadygo!

(*Hare dashes off—Down-Right! The others stare, appalled*).

DOG. He's gone the wrong way!

HEDGEHOG. Oh dear! Oh, dearie me!

DOG. He's going back!

HEDGEHOG. Oh my pins and needles!

DOG. He'll end up at the River Bank again!

HEDGEHOG. Mr. Sloe will win! Turn him back, Mr. Basket! Turn him back!

DOG. I'll try, but if he keeps up that speed, I'll never do it. What was in that egg!—Heh, Fleet! Fleet! You're going the wrong way!

(*He dashes off in pursuit*).

HEDGEHOG. Oh dear, oh dear! I don't know what Mr. Sett will have to say about all this! Whatever made Mr. Fleet make a mistake like that!

Number One Tabs close.

CONTINUITY SCENE FOUR:

Hare rushes across from Down-Left to exit Down-Right (or steps), and up the aisle, taking the reverse route of Continuity Three.

Dog follows breathlessly, calling on him to stop, turn back, etc.

Number One Tabs open on Scene 5.

SCENE 5. THE RIVER BANK AGAIN

The Fisherman is still asleep.

All is peaceful.

The Girls wander on from Left, disconsolate.

JACKIE *(Is upset because they've lost touch with Mr. Basket again).*

ROBIN *(Is tired: doesn't know where to look now).*

JACKIE *(Where are they, anyway?).*

ROBIN *(Thinks they should wake the Fisherman and ask).*

JACKIE *(You do it).*

ROBIN *(No, you).*

JACKIE *(Doesn't like to).*

ROBIN *(Dares her).*

JACKIE *(Shall she?).*

ROBIN *(Yes).*

After much to-ing and fro-ing, Jackie reaches the point of shaking the Fisherman's shoulder.

A little bell at the top of the rod rings sharply. The line runs out.

The Girls retreat.

The Fisherman wakes, and plays the line, exclaiming with excitement and anticipation.

He eventually reels in—an old boot.

He is furious, and turns to see the Girls stifling their giggles.

Rat's head pops up above the bank. He is chortling.

The Fisherman throws the boot from him, and re-baits the hook.

Rat's head goes down.

The line is cast. Almost immediately: another bite.

He reels in an old frying-pan.

Rat's head pops up.

The Fisherman hurls it away: rebaits.

Rat's head goes down.

Another bite. An old push-chair wheel.

Rat up.

The Fisherman stamps on it, and it is a good thing that we cannot understand human gobble-di-gook as some of the words are not quite nice.

40

The Young Ladies have covered their ears.

Still grumbling, he throws the rod down and decides to take solace in food.

He finds the sandwiches—pop—cake—gone; getting angrier each time. He accuses the Girls who make vehement denials.

He has no proof, and is waving his finger before their noses when Hare dashes on, and cannons into him, sending him sprawling.

Hare is up first, darting round in amazement).

HARE. Great hairy hind-legs—I'm going the wrong-way!

(He belts off, passing Dog who skids on.

The Fisherman rises, raging. He grabs his landing-net. Dog manages to halt and change direction. The Girls exclaim and give chase.

The Fisherman succeeds in getting the net over Mr. Basket's head, but Mr. B. doesn't take kindly to it. He tears round in a circle, and centrifugal force spins the Fisherman to the River's edge where he teeters, unbalanced.

Mr. Basket runs off, followed by the Girls.

The Fisherman topples into the River. There comes a most satisfactory, amplified splash.

Rat comes over the bank, crosses to the spot and peers down . . .

Number One Tabs close quickly.

CONTINUITY SCENE FIVE:

On the now familiar auditorium track.

Mr. Fleet rushes through, followed by Mr. Basket, followed by The Girls.

Number One Tabs open on Scene 6.

Scene 6. The Grassy Bank Again

Mr. Spiney is just sitting.

Mr. Fleet tears across.

HEDGEHOG.   Where . . . wha! . . . Mr. Fle . . .

(Mr. Basket tears across).

I say . . . wha! . . . who . . . eh . . .

(The Girls tear across).

Who! What . . . wait . . . I don't . . .

(He is alone again).

They've *all* been eating raw eggs!—Do you know, I do believe they must have found a clutch of eggs back there—perhaps a whole clutch of clutches!

(His little nose wrinkles avidly, and he sets off to explore, Down-Right).

Number One Tabs close.

Continuity Scene Six:

Tortoise enters from the Auditorium door furthest from the stage, and undulates on.

He is not visibly distressed although he does mop his brow, but without, however, faltering in his ponderous rhythm.

As he nears the stage, Number One Tabs open on Scene 7.

(If the interval is taken here, Continuity Six may be omitted.)

SCENE 7. MR. BRUSH'S TREE

Ground Row—distant hedge.

Centre—the Tree. It has a very wide trunk, well scarred with old initials, hearts and arrows and the like.

Squirrel is Right of the Tree, looking off Down-Right.

George and Maude, young rustic humans, are taking their first 'walk out.'

Maude enters first, demurely scuffing the ground. George follows a few paces behind. He picks up a stoutish stick and, with an effort, breaks it.

Squirrel starts, sees them, and disappears Up-stage of the Tree. In a flash his head pokes round the trunk some feet up, observing them.

Maude gazes at George admiringly.

MAUDE *(Thinks he's ever-so strong).*

GEORGE *(Is duly modest, but suggests she feel his biceps).*

MAUDE *(Does. O-oo!).*

(George hurls a stone into the far distance. Then he does a hand-stand—(a cart-wheel? . . . at least a few vigorous press-ups)

Maude isn't looking—but she is.

Squirrel is rather exasperated.

Tortoise enters Down-Right, sees the humans, and sinks to the ground.

Maude sits at the foot of the Tree, and commences to make a chain of flowers. George, to one side, digs the ground with his toe.

There is a bit of an impasse all round.

Finally, George catches Maude's eye and absentmindedly—he's only been thinking about it all day—sits by her.

And there they sit. Not even any gobble-di-gook.

A very concerned Squirrel at last takes a chance).

SQUIRREL. P-sst!

TORTOISE. That you, Mr. Brush?

SQUIRREL. Yes. I'm up here. I think it would be safe if you crept across very quietly.

TORTOISE. Are you sure? I don't want to land up in a strange garden.

SQUIRREL. I don't think this sort of human is very interested in gardening.

43

TORTOISE.   Well, if you're sure . . .

(He Indian-crawls on all fours across the stage. And we thought he was slow before!).

SQUIRREL.   Go ahead. I must say I'm surprised and quite delighted to see you here first. Where's Mr. Fleet?

TORTOISE.   I'm not sure. He tends to get diverted.

SQUIRREL.   Good luck. Only two more check points, and then the finish.

TORTOISE.   Thank you, Mr. Brush.

SQUIRREL.   Press on. They are a bother, this sort of human, but I've never seen them harm a Woodlander.

TORTOISE.   No?

SQUIRREL.   But they do terrible damage to my Tree.

TORTOISE.   Oh?

SQUIRREL.   They cut the bark to pieces. Mr. Basket says they are marking their names.

TORTOISE.   On a tree!

SQUIRREL.   Yes, with knives.

TORTOISE.   They are the oddest creatures, humans.

SQUIRREL.   As a matter of fact, I think these are what Mr. Basket calls 'Soppy Dates'. It's a word he got from his little female humans. They are a special kind, anyway.

TORTOISE.   They haven't moved—yet they must have seen me.

(He is three-quarter way across).

SQUIRREL.   I doubt it.

(George has a clasp-knife out, and is repeatedly throwing it into the ground).

TORTOISE.   I say, I don't like this! He has a weapon!

SQUIRREL.   I thought as much! It means he's going to start cutting my Tree any second! Oh, I do wish the young humans wouldn't cut trees and break branches and rob nests! They just don't think you know.

TORTOISE.   Well, I'm glad the knife is not for me.

SQUIRREL.   It's all right now. I should get on your hind legs.

TORTOISE.   Yes.

(He does so).

That's better: now I can break into a trot again.

(Well . . . all speed is comparative).

Goodbye for now, Mr. Brush. Thank you for your help.

(He is nearly off).

SQUIRREL. See you at the finish. Good show.

(George rises and starts carving a heart and arrow. Maude, quite oblivious—yeah!—chains on.

Hare dashes through the auditorium on to the set, and falls exhausted).

HARE. I'm here! Check me.

(He pants madly).

Oo! Ah! Ooo—what a run! Mr. Brush?

SQUIRREL. Here, Fleet.

HARE. Ah, up there, eh? Has old Fat-legs passed?

SQUIRREL. Mr. Sloe has just this minute gone.

HARE. That's all right. I've caught up. I knew I could. Can stop for a breather. Mind if I rest against your Tree?

(He turns to the Tree, and for the first time sees George and Maude. They take not the slightest notice of him, But . . . he does a cartoon nip behind the trunk. There he was: there he isn't. His head, now directly below Mr. Brush's, looks out and round).

HARE. Why didn't you warn me?

SQUIRREL. No need, they can't see you.

HARE. What are you? Some kind of nut! I nearly squatted on the long-haired one!

SQUIRREL. Wouldn't have made any difference. They've no senses, that sort. As a matter of fact, the long-haired one is sitting on Mr. Croaker at this very moment!

HARE. Old Froggy Croaker! What's he doing here?

SQUIRREL. Came to watch the Race go by.

HARE. A fine view of it he's going to get from there!

SQUIRREL. Talking of the Race, hadn't you better get cracking?

HARE. I can catch old Fat-legs anytime. Let's watch these two a bit. We Hares are very interested in manology.

SQUIRREL. What in trees, is that?

HARE. Study of the humans. They are very simple, of course—you can lift things from under their noses—but interesting.

(Dog arrives, breathless).

Dog. There you are! I'll give it to you, Fleet, you can certainly move when you do run. My poor little female humans are miles behind again—What's the hold-up now?

Hare. Just observing the antics of these humans.

Dog. Oh, Soppy Dates. No need to worry about them. Watch.

(He bounds up to Maude, and about George's legs. They carve and chain on: from time to time staring into each others eyes, and then turning away bashfully).

Heh, Soppy Dates! I'm here. Give us a pat, then. Throw a stick— I'll bite you! Have a piece out of your leg! G-rr!

(He returns to the others).

Oh, a real pair of Soppy Dates, these two! You see?—Reynard and his Horses and Hounds could charge through here. These humans wouldn't notice: not when they're like this.

Hare. Well, course me up the Downs! Blind as Bunnies!

(He moves to George and peers into his face).

How d'ye do!

(No reaction.

Maude has finished her chain, and puts it on her head.

She joins George who stands back from his handiwork.

More bashful simpers.

Mr. Fleet studies the markings).

Hare. What's this, then?

Dog. It'll be their names.

Hare. What for?

Dog. I don't know. It's just something Soppy Dates do.

Squirrel *(Joining them).* Well, I wish they wouldn't! My poor trees! How would they like it if we scratched our names on them!

(Maude and George re-sit).

Hare. She's squatted on him again!

Dog. On who?

Hare. One of the Frogs.

Squirrel. I hope he had the sense to get under a root.

Hare. What happens now?

Dog. You watch. This is the bit that makes my little female humans wag their tails.

Squirrel. They haven't got tails!

Dog. Just a saying. They do it with their mouths. It's called giggling. Watch.

(The Three Animals squat Up-stage above the Pair. The five heads are in a group: Hare Up-centre between George and Maude: He has squeezed between them and the tree-trunk).

George *(Suddenly asks Maude to give him a kiss).*

Maude *(Won't: and thinks he's awful!).*

George *(Go on).*

Maude *(Perhaps just one, then).*

(She proffers her cheek. George closes his eyes and plants a smacker on it).

Hare. What in bunny-burrows is he doing!

Squirrel. Washing her . . .?

Hare. Isn't she big enough to wash herself!

Dog. That's the tail-wagging bit.

Hare. But why does he do it?

Dog. Because she's pretty.

Hare. Pretty! That creature! She's got no proper nibbling teeth to start with!

Squirrel. And no tail!

Hare. Nor any ears worth mentioning!

Squirrel. She's as bald as old Croaker!—I do hope he's all right.

Hare. No fur at all except this bit of mane. Pretty! Old Fat-legs isn't what I'd call pretty, but compared with humans, he's beautiful!

Dog. Yes, but she's pretty to him. Only one human can possibly think that another human is pretty.

Hare. Well I'll be jugged! Pretty—these specimens!

(He leans between them to have a last incredulous examination just when, two pairs of eyes closed in ecstasy, they turn to exchange a mutual kiss.

Hare gets kissed on both cheeks.

He leaps up).

Jumping buck-rabbits—I've been washed!—That does it! No more manology for me. I'm off.

Squirrel. About time, too.

Dog. Mr. Sloe will be at the Cornfield by now. If you waste any more time, he's going to win.

HARE. Win! Him! Don't make me wag my tail! We Hares are not only the . . .

SQUIRREL. Oh, do go, Fleet!

HARE. I'm off. Give me a start.

DOG. Great Danes preserve us! On your mark. Ready—steady—Go!

(Hare exits at speed.

Poor Jackie and Robin: we hear their calls and whistles for Mr. Basket).

DOG. Me too. I'll be glad when this race is over. My little humans are very tired. It's time I took them home. See you.

(He goes).

(Squirrel climbs behind his Tree.

George kisses Maude's cheek. The Girls enter. They giggle quietly. They cough. George and Maude shoot to their feet, and leap apart).

JACKIE *(Excuses herself and asks have they seen a dog?).*

ROBIN *(A large, playful, brown—or whatever—dog?).*

GEORGE *(Hasn't seen any dog. Has Maude?).*

MAUDE *(No, she hasn't. Have they lost one?).*

JACKIE *(Yes: sort of).*

ROBIN *(They've been looking all day).*

MAUDE *(Is very sorry, but they haven't seen him).*

GEORGE *(Says that they will keep a sharp look out).*

JACKIE *(Is very sorry to have bothered them).*

ROBIN *(Thank them very much).*

MAUDE *(No bother).*

GEORGE *(We weren't doing anything important. Goodbye).*

MAUDE *(Hopes he'll turn up. Goodbye).*

JACKIE AND ROBIN *(Thanks again. Goodbye).*

(With a last look back and a suppressed giggle, they exit Down-Left.

George and Maude are back in square one—toe scuffing. But not for long.

Maude suddenly sits again.

Mr. Brush grimaces: 'Oh, no'! Poor old Froggy Croaker.

Number One Tabs close.

Continuity Scene Seven:

Tortoise enters the auditorium.

Hare runs in immediately, passes him, halts and returns to him.

He strolls ostentatiously by Tortoise's side.

HARE. Still think you can win, Fat-legs?

TORTOISE. A race is never won until it's lost.

HARE. You'll be telling me next that a carrot in the paw is worth two in the garden.

TORTOISE. I might well. We also have a saying at home—'Do not count your turtles before they are hatched.' Had you thought about that?

HARE. Frankly, no, old Egg-head. 'Hares not to reason why: Hares but to do them in the eye!'—Herrick.

TORTOISE. Herrick?

HARE. Bob-Bob Herrick—the finest of our harey poets—Ah well, it's a nice day for a stroll, but I'd better be getting on.

TORTOISE. Yes. And, if you'll take my advice, don't dawdle anywhere. Remember curiosity killed the cat.

HARE. Horse radish! Care to start me off?

TORTOISE. Certainly, if you wish.

> *(They are about two-thirds down the Theatre. Hare stops, and limbers up. Tortoise moves on. Between each word, he takes several steps; he is not deliberately holding up—it's just his speed of speech).*
>
> On . . .

HARE *(With whimsical superiority to those around him: although we can all hear).* He hasn't forgotten. It just takes the poor old thing a bit of time to articulate.

TORTOISE. . . . your . . .

HARE. I told you he'd get around to it. He'd be all right in Sunday School telling a story—you wouldn't get out until Friday!

TORTOISE. . . . marks.

HARE. Ah, now we're getting somewhere! I'd better think about it, I suppose. He'll give the 'Ready' in the next ten minutes.

TORTOISE. Ready.

> *(He has reached the Apron).*

HARE. There we are, what did I tell you! It's a good job he doesn't stutter.

(He calls out).

Right-o-, Flash—I'm ready.

TORTOISE. Steady.

HARE. 'Steady,' no less! If I stay 'Steady' any longer, I'll take root. This is it—any half-hour now, and we're off. Wait for it . . . wait for it . . .

TORTOISE *(Two-thirds across the stage).* Go!

HARE. We're off!

(He belts down the aisle, flies across the stage passing Tortoise, and off Down-Left).

Tortoise continues, and finally goes from view.

Number One Tabs open on Scene 8.

SCENE 8. THE CORNFIELD

Ground-row—a Stone Wall.

Centre—a stuke or bale of straw, with two others Up-stage of it, RC and LC.

All is peaceful.

From over the wall come the sounds of a flock of sheep engaged in desultory conversation. On differing frequencies, and over-lapping each other, we can make out some of the chit-chat. All the 'a' vowels are in triplicate.

VARIOUS SHEEP *(Off)*. Marvelous day, Martin.
    Marvelous.
    Ma-mma! Mamma-a-a!
    Drat that lamb! Here, darling.
    Ah, basking, Grandpa?
    Admiring the panorama, lad. Just admiring the panorama.
    Barbara! Barbara—don't stray too far!
    Yes, Ma.
    Fancy Agatha's Bartholomew being half-black!
    Mark! Where is that lamb? Mark!
    Here Ma, gamboling with Sam.
    Afternoon, Arthur. Balmy again.
    Balmy as Bath, Bartrum. Balmy as Bath.
    Pappa, Pappa—can we play in the straw?
    Nay, lad! Whatever would Farmer Black say!
    Ah, Pa-a-a! Etcetera-a-a- . . .

A raucous car-horn, door slams and human gobble-di-gook, off Left.

Silence over the wall: then:—

Alarm! Alarm! Mark! Barbara! Ma! Ma! Alarm! Mark! Ma! Back! Back! Barbara! Ma! Ma! A car—no harm! Ma! Ma! etc.

The Urban-Notcouths descend on the Cornfield. Mr. U-N in T-shirt and jockey cap: Mrs. U-N in eye-searing slacks—'slacks', no man-made fibre was ever intended for this strain.

Miss U-N, a teen-age peroxide brunette, and Master U-N. We can tell Brando from Sophia: Brando wears the three-inch heels and the hair net.

They express their various satisfactions with the Sylvan spot— and dump their gear. Picnickers!

Brando jumps over the stuke Up-Right, and wrecks it. He looks over the wall.

He says that there is a load of crazy sheep. He yells at them. He throws stones: throwing further as the panic stricken flock— we hear—rush down the hill.

51

Various Sheep (*wildly off*). 'Alarm! Alarm! Back! Back! Martin! Barbara! Paronoia, that's what it is! Martin! Ma! Ma! Go far! Far!!

Brando follows with a few 'Pows!' from his imaginary six-shooter, then joins the others who are going to eat—or have a quick 'Nosh-Up' as they are so quaintly phrasing it, if only we understood English—before pitching the tents.

The—perhaps it is a good word, at that—'Nosh' is spread. Sandwiches, cake, chocolate all tastefully wrapped in newsprint, tissue and polythene: all manner of tinned stuff which U-N Senior struggles to open; fruit; bottles of beer and pop. And, to prove how genteel we really all are, Mrs. U-N is issuing paper plates and napkins.

However, as these seem to stand between him and the actual 'Nosh,' Brando's first action is to skim the plates around the field, crumple the napkins into balls and kick them.

They all start and, as they don't want to fill their nice car with rubbish, throw the wrappings over their shoulders.

And so it goes on. Bottles, cans, paper, skins, cores: all are strewn in profusion during the Scene.

But back to the beginning . . .

Sophia can't eat without music: she can't do anything without music, if it comes to that, and, with a half stripped banana held delicately between her neon-pink tinted lips, tunes her transistor.

'If music be the food of love'—then this is the very stuff for a Nosh-Up.

The Young Urban-Notcouths dance. And even the Urban-Notcouth Seniors seem to derive some stimulous. The Tempo of noshing, discarding of hygienic wrappers, and handing out of goodies, speeds up.

Hare rushes on, and takes cover behind the RC stuke. He has not been seen. His head pops up to reconnoitre. He tip-toes in double-time to above the stuke LC. Up comes his head again.

The music and the dancing fascinate him. It was only by an oversight that he forgot to mention that Hares are the nimblest, the most rhythmic, indefatigable etc., etc. . . . But as we knew this from our animal books, and are about to see it proven beyond doubt, nothing is lost.

Mr. Fleet dances. He achieves a remarkable union of his own Moonlight pas de Hare and the current rave as executed by Sophia and Brando.

He is so 'sent' that he actually joins them. They are so 'sent' that he is accepted. In his turn, he absently takes and eats various delicacies which Mrs. U-N is handing up as they near her.

Mr. U-N is engrossed in food, drink and his paper.

There is a break in the programme and Mr. Fleet, first to reach a state of 'un-Sent,' nips behind a stuke.

The music re-starts, but Brando has seen something off Down-Right. He exits to re-appear struggling with Tortoise.

He dumps Tortoise on his back, helpless.

Brando pokes and prods. Sophia is 'sent' again. Mrs. U-N won't have anything to do with such a creature: she can't bear Wood-lice and Ear-wigs. Mr. U-N walks over, has a look, and returns. Mr. Fleet pops up, and is delighted. He does a 'boxer's' salutation.

Dog runs on: sniffs Tortoise and speaks to him, but this is not audible above the transistor.

Brando backs away and threatens him. Mr. U-N hurls a bottle.

Dog runs off Left. Brando plagues Tortoise anew.

Mr. Fleet reaches over the stuke and intercepts a cake intended for Sophia. Then a banana . . .

Mr. U-N sees this. He tells Mrs. U-N casually that he is just going to the car, picking up a tent sack on the way, and exits Down-Left.

Mr. Fleet intercepts a cup of pop.

Mr. U-N enters Up-Left, and creeps up on Mr. Fleet. A struggle and uproar in which Brando joins, and Mr. Fleet is in the bag. They tie the mouth. The bag thumps and jumps around a bit, but Mr. Fleet is well and truly trapped.

What with one thing and another, this rural spot now resembles a battle field—or a popular beach at the end of a fine Summer Sunday.

Dog leads on the Girls. They exclaim over the plight of Mr. Sloe, and while arguing—they are too incensed to be over-awed by the U-Ns—put him on his feet.

Whilst the discussion rages, Mr. Sloe resumes his old rhythm and exits Down-Left.

Farmer Black, carrying a shot gun, comes over the wall.

He takes command. His first action being to put the butt of his gun into the transistor.

He takes no back-gobble-di-gook from any of them.
It is a monologue. He tells the Un-Ns that:—
   they are trespassing
   they've frightened his sheep
   they've no respect for the Country Code
   they have disgusting habits
   and he'll give them two minutes to clear up the mess!

The U-Ns set to, prompted and threatened by the Farmer.
Every last little toffee paper: every last straw back on its bale.

Finally: what's in this sack?

The sack convulses. Poaching too! Open it!

Mr. U-N unties the neck, and out shoots Mr. Fleet. Twice round, between Mr. U-N's legs, and knocking Brando down, he gets direction, and darts off Down-Left.

Mr. Basket follows.

The Girls, with a word to Farmer Black, run too.

Farmer Black, gun in support, is going to prosecute.

Got a car, have they? Good. It'll save a walk to the village Police Station.

On the litter-laden and dejected exit of the Urban-Notcouths . . .

Number One Tabs close.

CONTINUITY SCENE EIGHT:

Tortoise is crossing the Apron from Left to Right.

Hare passes him, turns and runs backwards pulling 'fat-bacon' at him.

They are going to exit through the auditorium via a previously untravelled aisle, if we still have one.

Half-way up Mr. Fleet again delivers himself: this time of:—

HARE. Not only am I the nimblest and most graceful dancer of all the Woodlanders, but I am the most dexterous escapologist . . . The trap has yet to be invented that can hold me . . . Hares laugh at Snares! . . . Ah well, I'd better saunter to the winning post. If you're still here when old Fat-legs totters past, give the old thing a cheer or two. He's trying his best.

Ta-ta. Here we go again. Will you start me off?

(If our Hare has so alienated our affections, he may have to call his own start, but we doubt it. Some, if not all of us, will oblige with 'On your marks etc.'—and off he goes.

Tortoise storms in pursuit, to thunderous encouragement).

On his exit, Number One Tabs open on Scene 9.

54

SCENE 9. THE COTTAGE GARDEN

This time the Ground Row is Down-stage. It is the Stone Wall.

Above it, in the Garden, stretching across the stage with no visible supports other than a central prop, is a washing line.

Mrs. Stainer, a buxom good-wife, is hanging out her wash. She wears thick glasses.

The job complete, towels, shirts and what-not flapping gently, she exits.

Mr. Fleet, at a comfortable lope, enters Down-Right.

Centre, a familiar scent strikes his nostrils.

HARE. Carrots!
(He peers over the wall).

O-oo, beauties! Young and tender.

(He whistles nonchalantly; walks, cranes and looks).

Nobody guarding them. Very remiss. If I grew carrots like that I should watch them night and day. If people don't guard their carrots, they jolly well deserve to lose them.

(He looks over again).

Wouldn't take two minutes. Old Fat-legs is way behind—and this is the last point. Better just make sure he hasn't got a lift on a hay-wagon. Sort of mean trick he would get up to.

(He looks off Right).

No, not out of Nobbet's Spinney yet. Not only are we Hares in general, and myself in particular, the fastest, most intelligent and prettiest of the Woodlanders, but I am also the agilest vaulterer-rer of garden walls in the country.

(He has several dummy attempts employing different approaches, none of which look like being successful. So . . .).

I might damage the carrots if I land on them from too great a height.

(He climbs the wall. Even now his second leg is caught, and he falls inelegantly from view. However, his head soon pops up. He is eating a carrot).

Delicious!

(He bobs down.

Mr. Basket enters, hot on the trail. Sniffing, he follows Mr. Fleet's confusing tracks; realizes that he has not gone through: returns to Centre and starts a prolonged exploration of the wall. Mr.

55

Fleet, looks over, munching, and surveys him. Their faces meet. Basket leaps back).

Dog. What in old slippers are you doing there!

Hare. Vitamins. Very good for the eye-sight. Have one. Oh, there are only six left. Sorry.

Dog. The old female human here will give you vitamins if she catches you.

Hare. She can't see for bilberries. I expect that's why she has grown these perfectly delectable carrots.

Dog. You're supposed to be in a Race! Not stopping stealing carrots.

Hare. Race! I could hop on one leg from here and win! As a matter of fact, I think I will—would be very spectacular. Not only do I run, dance and box magnificently, but I am quite the hottest hopper-rer in the kingdom.

Dog. You're quite the loudest boasterer-rer!

Hare. Please—no petty envy.

Dog. Well, you'd better hop back quick—here's the old female human!

Hare *(Choking).* What!
(He makes an ineffective scramble, falls back, panics).

Dog. Quick! Come on! She'll catch you!

(Mr. Fleet fails again. What to do?

He runs to a gap between the clothes on the line and, fore-legs stretched in a Y holding the line he 'makes-like' a piece of washing.

Mrs. Stainer works down the line from Left feeling each piece to see if it is dry.

Mr. Basket ducks below our side of the wall.

Mr. Fleet trembles.

Mrs. Stainer puts extra pegs in a towel. She reaches Mr. Fleet, and feels him. It tickles: one 'leg' involuntarily lets go of the line. Repeat.

She thinks this is a bit rum, and pegs it securely: then the other 'leg,' and finding his ears dangling—pegs those too.

She completes her examination, and re-adjusts the prop. Singing rurally, she exits Left.

Mr. Fleet is spread-eagled on tip paw.

Mr. Basket cautiously stands against the wall and looks over).

Dog. Fleet? Fleet—you all right?

Hare. No, I'm not all right! Get me down!

Dog. Where are you?

Hare. Here!

Dog. Where? I can smell you, but I can't see you.

Hare. You're looking straight at me, bat eyes!

(He wriggles).

Here!

Dog. Behind the washing?

Hare. I *am* the washing! The third shirt from the left!

Dog. Ye Danes and little litters! This is no time to be drying yourself off. Come down!

Hare. I can't come down! I'm pegged up! Lower the line. Unpeg me quick!

Dog. How can I lower lines? I couldn't unpeg you, anyway.

Hare. You domesticated, bottle-fed, hand-reared, kennel-housed renegade from the real animals! I'll see that you don't play in our Woods any more!

Dog. Now don't get shirty—as my little female humans would say. Likewise: keep your hair on!

Hare. Well, do something! Quick—here's Fat legs! He'll win! He'll win!

(Mr. Sloe crosses from Down-Right).

Dog. Heh, Torto! It's Mr. Fleet in trouble again. He's fastened to the clothes line.

Tortoise. Oh dear. What is he now—the whiter than white Rabbit?

Hare. Get me down! Stop! Not fair to Hare!

Dog. Can you help, Torto?

Tortoise. Sorry, I really cannot stop this time. Only two fields to the finishing post. Must keep moving. Can't win races if you stop.

(He leaves the stage, and is on his way up an aisle).

Hare. I've been framed!

Dog. My little female humans call it being taken to the cleaners. I never did understand what they meant before.

Tortoise *(Calling back from the auditorium).* You'd best fetch them, Mr. Basket. They could get him down.

Dog. My little female humans. Of course!

Hare. They'd put me in a hutch!

Dog. Not they. They won't keep any animal that prefers the woods. I'll find them.

(He exits Down-Right).

Hare. Hurry! It's the last lap!

(He yells after the retreating Tortoise).

I'll catch you! You can't beat me! You see—as soon as I am free, I'll catch you up and win by a mile . . . Hare will be there!

(Tortoise leaves us, well on his way).

I'll show him! This is the return I get for letting him keep up with me! And offering him a start! And distracting those humans in the Cornfield so that he could get away!—Some animals can only win by cheating!

(Mr. Basket enters and paws the wall. The Girls follow).

Dog. Here we are, then. Come on, little friends, look where I'm pointing.

Jackie *(Wonders what's up with Mr. Basket).*

Robin *(Thinks he's trying to show them something).*

Jackie *(Perhaps a cat in the garden).*

Robin *(He knows he's not to chase cats. He must come down).*

Dog. Oh, come on! Come on! You're not usually so slow as this. Look—hanging up like a piece of washing! Hare. Third shirt from the left.

Jackie and Robin. ?

Hare. You mole-eyed, cow-snouted, fly-brained little human sub-does—I'm here! Get me down!

Dog. It's no use you screeching like that: they can't understand you.

(But they have heard).

Jackie *(Is startled. She looks and points).*

Robin *(Can it be? It is—a hare, pegged to the line!).*

Dog. That's it! You've seen him! Get him!

(He shouts and bounds against the wall).

Robin *(Says he is to get down. He is a bad dog. He is not to touch the poor hare. She cuffs him).*

Dog. Ow! Ow! Ow-ow!

Hare. You all right?

Dog. Yes. She thinks I want to chase you. Fine thing getting a clip when you're just trying to help!

JACKIE *(Thinks it's terribly cruel. What can they do?).*

ROBIN *(Set him free, of course).*

JACKIE *(How? Old Mrs. Stainer might see).*

ROBIN *(Has an idea).*

JACKIE *(Yes. Who is going to do what?).*

HARE.   What are they on about?

DOG.   Making a plan. One of them is going to ask the old female human for a drink of water, and then the other one is going to climb over and set you free.

HARE.   Well, I wish they'd HURRY!

JACKIE *(Poor thing, he's in terrible pain! Listen).*

ROBIN *(She'll tackle Mrs. Stainer).*

JACKIE *(All right, she'll go over the wall).*

DOG.   Won't be long now.

   (Robin takes a deep breath and exits Down-Left. Mr. Basket follows to the wings. Jackie watches and waits.

   We hear a knock and faint conversation. Mr. Basket returns to Centre).

   Go on, now. She's busy at the door.

JACKIE *(Tells him to be quiet. She essays the climb).*

HARE.   Just as I thought. About as athletic as a worm!

DOG.   Quiet. She's doing her best.

JACKIE *(Ss-sh. He's a bad dog! Mr. Basket implores the Heavens.*

   He puts his back conveniently under a dangling foot and bunks her over.

   The next few minutes are hectic.

   Jackie scrambles to the prop and lowers the line fully. The clothes and Mr. Fleet disappear for a moment. Then up he comes, still attached to the line, squirming.

   There is some furious milling around as Jackie pulls the pegs.

   Mr. Basket keeps cave on the Cottage Door (Off Left).

HARE.   About time—Ow—my ear! The other peg!

JACKIE *(Is telling him to keep quiet, and that she won't hurt him).*

DOG *(At the wall).* Shut up, Fleet, and stay still. The old female human will hear.

   (Robin rushes back, speaking).

Quick! She says the old female human has gone in to see to the washing!

(Mr. Fleet is free. He scales the wall, and is off up the aisle . . . Jackie lifts the line on the prop, and scrambles back to our side).

The clothes are in a shocking state: soiled, crumpled and paw-marked. (Second pre-set line).

Mrs. Stainer has appeared. She exclaims over the debacle.

The Girls and Mr. Basket huddle at the foot of the wall.

Mrs. Stainer just glimpses the bobbing tail of Mr. Fleet on his way out.

She shouts and gesticulates, and exits Left to re-enter immediately with a shot-gun.

She blazes away over our heads, as . . .

Number One Tabs close.

Continuity Scene Nine:

The furthest auditorium door bursts open and Mr. Sloe enters the stadium.

Down he comes, but not one whit faster than previously.

He is about half-way down when . . .

Number One Tabs open on Scene 10.

Scene 10. Frog Rock Quarry Again

Present All the Animals (except possibly Water Rat who, if he has been playing Mrs. Stainer, may be a little late)—plus any Cubs, Does, Leverets etc., who may have come to see the Finish of the Great Cross Country Race.

They all raise a tremendous cheer as they spot Mr. Sloe.

BADGER.   Well done, Mr. Sloe! Well done indeed!

ROOK.   Encore! Encore!

SQUIRREL.   Splendid fellow! Come on, keep it up!

RABBIT.   I am surprised!

RAT *(Or who-ever)*.   Come on, old Sloe! Come on!

HEDGEHOG.   Thunder on, Mr. Sloe! Thunder on!

BADGER.   Once round the quarry, and you're home!

SQUIRREL.   Where's Hare?

HEDGEHOG.   He's not in sight yet! He's not in sight!

RABBIT.   I'm quite dizzy with excitement!

SQUIRREL.   I said he could do it! Stout fellow!

BADGER.   One last effort, Mr. Sloe.

ROOK.   Hoo-raw! Hoo-raw! *(And so on . . .*
Mr. Sett displays the back of the gate on which is chalked Last Lap with an arrow pointing Right.

Mr. Sloe reaches the stage from Left, and continues to exit Right and start on a complete tour of the auditorium—the stadium lap).

RAT.   Just once round the Quarry, and you're home!

RABBIT.   Oh, do hurry, Mr. Sloe!

ROOK.   Once more! Once more!

HEDGEHOG.   He's still not in sight! You're going to win!

SQUIRREL.   Young Fleet licked at last! Go on, Sloe!

BADGER.   We'll get out the tape. Keep it up!

(Mr. Sloe is approaching the back-straight).

RABBIT.   Hurry!

ROOK.   Hoo-raw!

HEDGEHOG.   Hare's nowhere!

Squirrel. Keep it up!

Rat. Faster, Mr. Sloe. Put on a spurt!

Badger. Run up! Run up!

Hedgehog. Hare couldn't do it even if he came now!

Squirrel. Go, Sloe, go! You're home and dried!

Rat. Only half a lap to go!

Rabbit. Quickly! Quickly!

Badger. On, on, on!

Hedgehog. More speed!

Rook. More! More!

Squirrel. It's in the bag!

Rabbit. E-eee! He's here!

> (*Mr. Fleet crashes in at tremendous rate. He simply flies down the aisle whizzing past Mr. Sloe, who is, of course, on his last few yards.*
>
> *The din is terrific. All the Animals repeating what they've said and ad-libbing—which we will drown anyway with our own support.*
>
> *Mr. Fleet rushes on, breasts the tape—only it isn't being held out yet—heroically, and collapses just managing a Victor's hand-clasp.*
>
> *Mr. Sloe lumbers relentlessly on.*
>
> *They all yell together . . .).*

Badger. There's another lap! You haven't finished!

Hedgehog. Round the Quarry again!

Squirrel. Another lap! Run, Fleet, run!

Rabbit. Oh! Oh! Oh! I think I'm going to faint!

Rat. Go on! Again! You can just make it!

Hedgehog. Round again!

Rabbit. Hurry! Oh, do hurry!

Rook. I implore! I implore!

Badger. You must finish the course! Round again!

Squirrel. Up, Fleet up!

> (*Truth dawns on Mr. Fleet—and off he goes.*
>
> *Mr. Sloe is mounting to the stage.*

Mr. Sett and Mr. Brush hold the tape taut).
Come on, Fleet.

HEDGEHOG. Come on, Sloe!

RABBIT. Come on, Somebody!

BADGER. Run up! Run up!

ROOK. A draw! A draw!

(And it nearly is . . . but Mr. Sloe surges into the tape—First: as Mr. Fleet bursts past him—Second.

He again collapses, this time into the arms of Mr. Paddle and Mr. Spiney. He is trying to utter protests and objections and explain the dire plots that have delayed him. But he hasn't the breath to be intelligible and they are all talking at once again, anyway).

BADGER. Mr. Sloe wins!

SQUIRREL. Great show, Sloe, Congratulations!

TORTOISE. Thank you. Thank you!

HEDGEHOG. The Winner!—Hold up, Mr. Fleet.

RABBIT. Mr. Sloe wins! Mr. Sloe wins! Oh—I'm quite dizzy!

ROOK. Hoo-raw! Hoo-raw!

RAT. I thought he'd do it. Very well run, Mr. Sloe—You feeling all right, Mr. Fleet?

BADGER. What a splendid race!

HEDGEHOG. You must challenge Mr. Reynard now.

TORTOISE. That would be very different, I feel.

SQUIRREL. Mrs. Dark, let all the Woodlanders know.

ROOK. Sure, sure.

HEDGEHOG. They will be surprised.

BADGER. You'll join me for a bite of tea, Mr. Sloe?

TORTOISE. If you'll excuse me, Mr. Sett, I really must get back to the garden. It has been most enjoyable.

BADGER. I quite understand.

HEDGEHOG. We ought to get Mr. Fleet a drink. He's quite exhausted.

SQUIRREL. He'll revive.

BADGER. A worthy Woodland Champion.

TORTOISE. Any of you could have done it. I'm afraid our young friend lacks concentration.

SQUIRREL. Grass Hopper minded.

HEDGEHOG. Won't stick at things.

RAT. Too easily diverted. Always said so.

RABBIT. But he can run fast.

(*Mr. Basket reaches the stage from the auditorium*).

DOG. Here I am. Who won?

BADGER. Mr. Sloe—by a neck.

DOG. Good old Torto! Three cheers for Mr. Sloe. Hep, hep—etc.

(*The Animals, especially if there are young ones, dance and sing "Thunder on," altering the lyric to 'We are glad that you were there, at the post before the Hare!*

The Girls enter the Auditorium).

ROOK. Warning! Warning! Withdraw! Withdraw!

(*The Animals freeze as previously, with the exception of Mr. Fleet who has had a relapse. He lies on his back, panting and kicking feebly.*

The Girls reach the stage).

DOG. It's all right, they won't hurt. I've just brought them to pick up Mr. Sloe. Come on, you two, here's your pet.

(*He sniffs Mr. Sloe, who emerges*).

JACKIE (*Why, here he is! Clever dog!*).

ROBIN (*Here all the time! This is where they started!*).

JACKIE (*Thinks it would be wise to tie his string on and lead him*).

ROBIN (*Yes*).

(*She sees the prostrate Hare. They both bend over him compassionately*).

JACKIE (*Poor thing! Nearly run himself to death!*).

ROBIN (*That terrible Mrs. Stainer, tying him to a washing line!*).

HARE. What are they saying?

DOG. That you're a poor weak animal who's run himself to death because you were frightened.

HARE. They are probably right!

DOG. And that you are squeaking with terror. Now they are planning to take you home and keep you in a hutch.

HARE. I knew it!

DOG. And feed you on bread and milk.

HARE. I hate bread and milk!

DOG. Then take my advice—nip off quick.

(Jackie cuffs him, and tells him not to worry the poor hare).

Ow! She's done it again! Every time I talk to you, I get a smack! —Go on, hop it! I'll give you a start. On your mark—Ready. Steady Go!

(Mr. Fleet goes with what alacrity he can muster.

The Girls are relieved. He can't be so ill, and it's for the best— But Basket is a bad dog for frightening him).

DOG. I didn't frighten him! Oh dear, you're very nice but I wish sometimes you had the sense to understand what I say.

(Robin speaks to him, and pulls his lead).

No, I won't stop barking! Barking! I'm talking to my friends— Cheerio, all of you. Been a grand days sport. What's on to-morrow?

BADGER. We're not sure yet. But Mr. Paddle thinks we should have the Swimming Gala.

DOG. Good idea!

BADGER. We're meeting on the River Bank.

DOG. Right. We'll be there.

—(To Robin who is yanking him off).

All right, love, don't choke me! I'm coming—Bye, all.

(A little chorus of 'Goodbyes'

The Animals start to uncurl.

The Girls turn back: they freeze again—the Girls exit and the Curtain Falls).

CURTAIN CALL

The Curtain Rises on the same still picture.

In order, Mrs. Dark—Mrs. Warren—Mr. Paddle—Mr. Spiney— Mr. Brush uncurl and take a bow.

Mr. Basket runs on to Centre, and bows.

Jackie and Robin join him and bow.

Mr. Sloe runs—at speed—from Left.

Mr. Fleet enters from Right—on crutches.

All wave 'Goodbye' and the hair-raising adventures of the Hare and the Tortoise are over for another night.

PRODUCTION NOTES

Stylization of settings and costume is not only the simplest form of presentation, but also the most effective.

A pleasantly lighted Sky-cloth, and Neutral Wings stand throughout.

The Ground-rows—hard-board cut-outs on light frames—which are rested against the base of the Sky-cloth, are a feature. Made in two or three lengths, they must be easily portable.

If painted on both sides, three will suffice:—

    1. Boulders (Sc. 1, 10) River Bank (Sc. 3, 5)
    2. Hedge (Sc. 2, 7)
    3. Wall (Sc. 8, 9—stage-braced, and rostrum backed)

The Centre pieces vary, but involve only the simplest construction and handling.

The whole painted in bold 'picture book' convention.

SCENE 1. Ground-row of boulders as in an abandoned quarry. A few other boulders for the Animals to *merge* with would help, but they must NOT hide behind them. The reverse side of the Grassy Bank could be used.

The Centre Piece is a dominant cut-out vaguely resembling a frog.

SCENE 2. Ground-row—rough hedge and brambles.

The Centre piece is best made from four twiggy but stout branches about 3' 6" high set in wood blocks, themselves set on a square board about 3' x 3'. The Down-stage blocks are hinged on their outside edges: strong elastic joins them. This allows them to give sufficiently for Hare to get well into the centre of the 'Thicket.' It must be able to stand rough treatment, otherwise the struggling business will be thin and ineffective. The whole painted, and canvas leaves wired on.

SCENE 3. Ground-row—edge of the River (reverse of boulder ground-row).

Two mounds of solid bank—again the Grassy Bank should be one of them—are essential. One for Water Rat's use: the other for the Fisherman's fall.

No centre piece.

SCENE 4. If a Central Traverse is available, no Ground-row is needed.

The Centre Piece—the Bank—is all that is necessary. As we have to alternate between the River and the Grassy Bank, and if no Number Two Traverse Curtain exists, then it would be expedient to place the Bank below Number One Tabs, or even the House Tabs (assuming a small Apron Stage below them) rather than strike and re-set the River.

In this case, Continuity Scenes 3 and 4 are played on the auditorium floor.

SCENE 7. Ground-row—undergrowth (Reverse of Scene 2).

Centre Piece, the Tree Trunk. A really wide hard-board cut-out.

The smallest stage has room to fly a little 'tree' (leaf) border. This is lowered in to give the lower branches and leaf spread of what is a huge tree rising out of our vision. On the trunk are pre-cut initials and hearts covered by adhesive tape which George strips off whilst carving. A pair of steps up-stage of the trunk for Squirrel.

SCENE 8. Ground-row—Stone Wall about 4' 6".

Centre Piece. Actual bales of straw or hay are ideal: otherwise cut-outs.

The Voices of the Flock. A large company, especially if using extras, will have no difficulty with this 'noises off.' A small cast would be advised to tape the effect.

In either case, the *intelligible speech element* must come over, or our agreed convention of animals—understood: humans— not understood, falls down.

SCENE 9. Ground-row—the Stone Wall Down-stage. A couple of weighted table or rostra supports above it are necessary, or, again, the full physical business will be impractical.

The Centre Piece—the Washing Line. This is attached to the wing walls, and the line traverses the width of the acting area. A second line with identical but soiled clothes is pre-set. On cue, the Girl hoists number 2 instead of number 1.

Before Scene 10, the Animals and Young Animals (with the exceptions of Badger and Rook) may come through the Auditorium from various entrances. They are making their way back to Frog Rock for the Finish.

It must be played, even to the extent of their asking individual Children "Whom do you want to win?" "We must hurry—they'll be here in a minute" etc.

The Children enjoy this: it does allow extra time if necessary for the Cottage/Frog Rock change, and it raises expectancy.

As the Curtain rises on Frog Rock, Badger calls on them to hurry, and they flow on to the set—as Tortoise enters at the rear.

———

The timing of the Continuity Sequences and final 'lap' can only be worked to the physical auditorium. Producers may delete or insert lines, and alter indicated entrances and positions to suit. The whole of the Technical side of this play has been planned to allow for simple, effective management which can be elaborated to company resources. Similarly, the casting may be—within reasonable limits—flexible.

The Human Speech—Gobble-di-gook.

In the original production Back Slang, or Dog Latin, was used most effectively, and is recommended to any Company which has a member or associate who knows its simple formula, and who could instruct.

(The initial letter or sound is placed at the end of the word, and EH added. Small words beginning with a vowel: merely add the EH.

Thus:—'Basket, Basket, where are you? Here, boy. Good dog. Would be:—'Askitbeh, Askitbeh, erewhey areh ouyeh? Ereheh oybeh. Oodgeh ogdeh.' etc.)

Another idea would be to use a foreign language such as French in an English production: English to a young French audience. It is important that the Gobble-di-gook has some linguistic discipline, otherwise a slack and dreary succession of vowel sounds will result in an unauthentic speech form.

Designed by
IRENE COREY

Photographs: Jerry Mitchell
Projection Consultant: James Hull Miller

(Hare and Tortoise: Modeled by Dorothy Bradley)

HEDGEHOG
(Modeled by Mary Ann DeNoon)

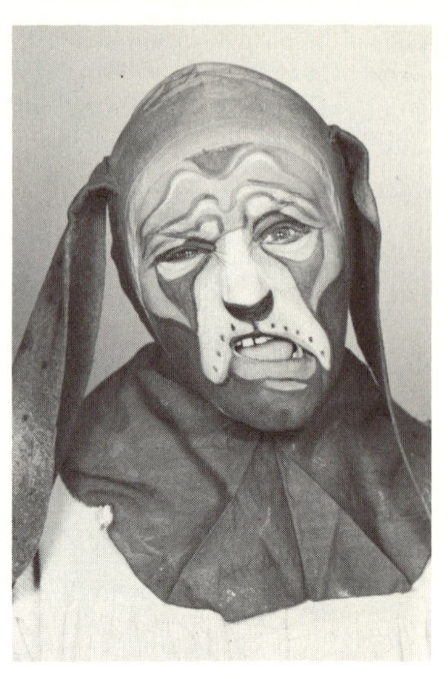

DOG
(Modeled by Dorothy Bradley)

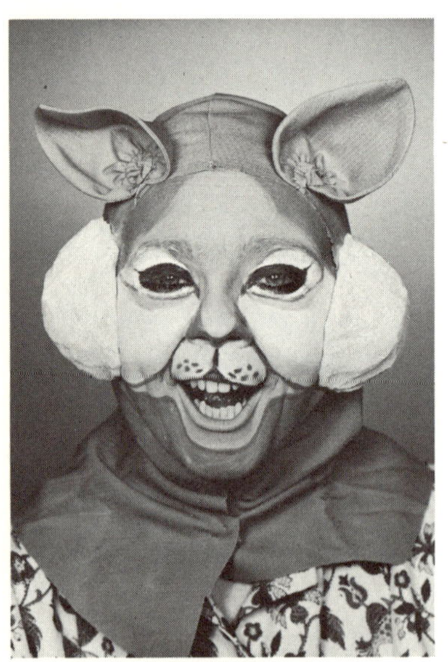

SQUIRREL
(Modeled by Barbara McMillian)

BADGER
(Modeled by Paula Stahls)

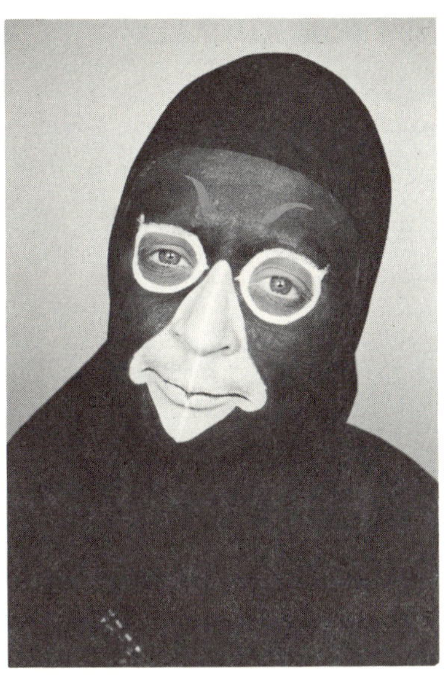

ROOK
(Modeled by Mary Ann DeNoon)

RAT
(Modeled by Jeannie Marlin Smith)

RABBIT
(Modeled by Barbara McMillian)

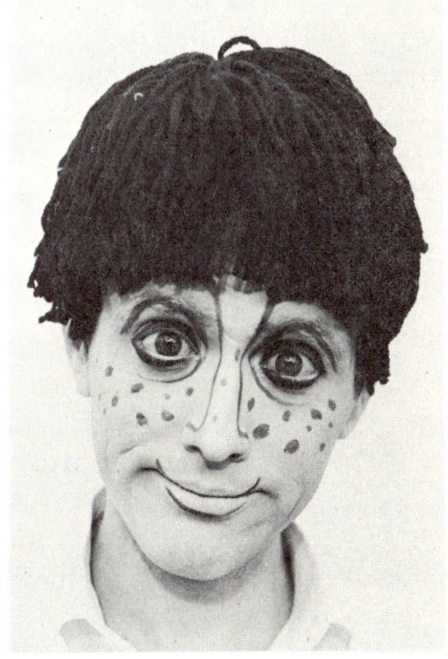

GEORGE
(Modeled by Allen Shaffer)

All numbers given with the make-up charts refer to Stein's Stick greasepaint. Greasepaint requires the application of cold cream first. Wipe off thoroughly.

Use soft bristled brushes, flat, 3/16 inch. Lipstick brushes will serve.

Put on the wimple head-piece first. Draw a line around the edge, on face. Remove the wimple, and use the line as a guide for edges of makeup, extending beyond this boundary about ½ inch toward hair line.

Always outline all areas and the eyes with a medium tone. Then hold the design beside the face, and compare in the mirror. Make all corrections at this point. Notice the position of areas and lines in relation to the human features. We all have two eyes, a nose and a mouth, (so do animals) but we do not look alike. The subtle shifting of a line distinguishes a rabbit from a squirrel; a mouse from a marmot.

For mixing the area colors, use a regular artist's paper palette, or any smooth firm surface, and mash grease paint with a regular table knife. Mix and blend the colors thoroughly. Test on the back of the hand for color, remembering that the color comes through the intensity, not the thickness of application. Store in plastic pill bottles. In mixing, the point is always to blend areas closest to wimple with the color of the fabric. If the shade of your wimple requires the addition of other colors, add them.

Plain white talcum powder seems to leave the colors the purest. Holding a tray under your chin, use a large puff, and liberally coat the face till it is white. Let it set one or two minutes, and brush off carefully with a complexion brush. Start with the lighter areas.

For extra sharp blacks and whites, and the red eye accents, liquid makeup can be used after powdering.

Sponge rubber or net cheek poufs may be glued to cheeks after powdering, if they need it. If the wimple fits tightly enough, it will not be necessary.

GENERAL COSTUME NOTES FOR ANIMALS

On the art of being an animal

The whole idea behind going to so much work to create an animal by means of makeup and costume will be lost if the actor does not spend some time studying the movement characteristics of the real animal. Without these distinguishing traits, the actor becomes merely a man in an animal suit, and if he is going to portray a man, then why not wear a man's suit? The zoo is the most obvious place to study the animals. If this is impossible, at least look them up in the encyclopedia to learn about their habits.

The art of being an animal usually involves the wearing of a tail. Unfortunately, tails are a foreign element to humans, and as they have to be intricately rigged to resemble nature, some new habits must be learned. The actor cannot be directed to sit against anything, or lie on his back, either on stage or off stage.

BASIC CONSTRUCTION NOTES

Wimples:

As all the heads of the animals are formed on a wimple, that basic construction is given here:

To arrive at a wimple pattern pin two pieces of fabric (approximately ½ yard each), together over the crown of the head, and under the chin. Mark pinned line with chalk. Draw a line along hair line at front and temples, down and under the chin. Take piece off, and lay them flat. Correct the lines into a smooth curve. Allow for seams. The amount the wimple dips down over the forehead is determined by the animal design. Do cover the hairline well. Allow about 8 inches from base of neck out over shoulders. The shape at the bottom depends on the animal design. Bind the face edge with bias tape.

Sew straight extensions on under chin openings. Overlap and mark for hooks or velcro. The wimple should fit very snugly around face. Elastic may be used, if necessary. For fitted neck, make darts on sides.

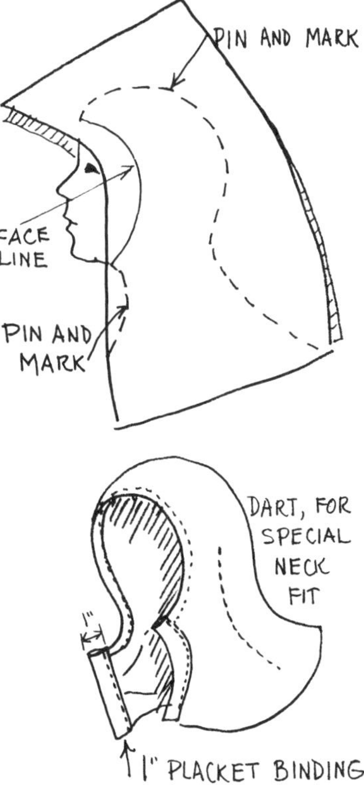

T-Shirts:

Except where specified, get the large loose fitting t-shirts. This serves to conceal the human figure, lending more readily to the animal shape. In all instances, the t-shirts are the long sleeved variety.

For ease in getting shirts on and off, over makeup, it is advisable to put long zippers in the back of them. In most cases, the turtle neck can be cut off; and the neck bound. Place a 5 inch strip of matching cotton down center back, on the outside. Machine stitch down the center; turn, and return up the same line of stitching, about 1/8 inch away. Cut between rows of stitching, and turn facings to the wrong side. Tack facings down. Put right sides of shirt together, and make a seam, about one inch wide, on long stitch. On one side of seam allowance, baste a tiny fold as close as possible to the stitching line. With zipper right side up, stitch along fold to one side of zipper. Lay shirt flat, with right side down. Turn zipper so that its back side is up. Stitch down other side, keeping seam pulled open. Take out long stitches. Hook at the top.

Shoes:

If you plan to produce the play only a few times, the sock feet will wear well enough. However, if you plan a long run, it will be advisable to build the animal feet over soft slippers. The best kind for this is the leatherette moccasin style Jiffie l.ouse slipper, because it has an edge extending out from the sole on which the sock can be fastened. The sole is soft, and can be sewed through easily. The soft, folding T V slippers will work, if they have the edge extending at the sole.

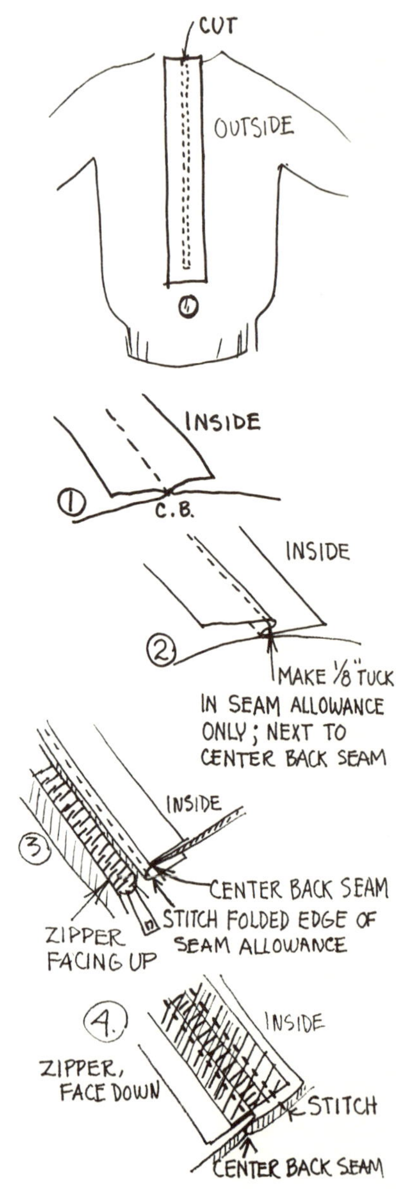

Supplies:

Be certain when substituting for materials suggested. In every case, the fabrics have been chosen because of some particular quality. For example: Jersey for the tortoise, because it must drape; Net for the hedgehog because its ruffles appear prickly; Organdy for its crispness and transparency, etc. Dacron batting is suggested rather than cotton, because it is lighter, does not tend to wad and lump, and is more resilient. No other wire has the same quality that millinery wire has. It is stiff, holds its shape, yet can be easily bent with pliers. Only hoop wire (such as is used in hoop skirts) will form a pliable, perfect circle, bouncing back into shape when it is hit.

For those who do not have ready access to theatrical supplies, the following sources are suggested:

Stein's grease paint Liquid makeup Makeup brushes	Paramount Theatrical Supplies Alcone Co., Inc. 32 West 20th St. New York 11, N. Y.
Hoop wire Millinery wire Tights White maribou No. 0895	Dazian's 142 West 44th St. New York, N. Y.

T-shirts (light weight, cotton knit
   long sleeved, turtle neck)
Indicate color choice; list white as
   alternate, and dye
	S. M. Rich Textiles Inc.
	1016 6th Ave.
	New York 18, N. Y.

Jumbo size hooks and eyes, size 6	Lew Serbin, Inc. 222 Powell Street San Francisco 2, Calif.
Jiffies (house slippers)	All Large Department Stores and Men's Stores
Dacron batting	Sears, Roebuck Catalogue

COSTUME FOR MRS. WARREN, A RABBIT

Materials:

T-shirt: yellow-brown, large size

Tights: yellow-brown

Socks: yellow-brown, two pair large men's size

Fabrics: yellow-brown cotton, for wimple, ears and belly; orange velveteen, for ear lining; brown net, for belly, tail and cheeks; brown felt, for pads on paws; muslin, for paws; stiff interlining, cheek pads

Twill tape

Hoop wire

Nylon line

Desired Effect:

Mrs. Warren confesses that she is "much too matronly" for some of the sports, so in contrast to the skinny hare she is made up of happy curves. Shorter, rounder ears; pudgy cheeks; and a fluffy, jovial tummy create a sense of well-fed prosperity. From her fat paws to her fluffy chops she should be a thumping, bumping bundle of good will.

Basic Garments:

The t-shirt should be large. Shirt, tights, socks and cotton for wimple can be purchased in white and dyed yellow-brown all at one time.

Body:

Fit t-shirt on actor. Fasten hoop wire to sides of t-shirt. Let it bell out in front to form stomach. Attach twill tape from shirt to center front of hoop to hold it level.

Measure from neck, over hoop to bottom of t-shirt (just above knit band at lower edge of shirt). Cut a length of brown cotton and a length of net by this measurement. Gather net and cotton, as one piece of fabric, at top and bottom. Fit over hoop, tucking under raw edges and corner. Sew to shirt.

Tail:

Cut seven widths of brown net into strips 14 inches wide. (Net can be folded and cut through many thicknesses at one time). Net is two yards wide. Cut these pieces in two, making them one yard long. Through seven thicknesses, by hand, run a gathering thread made of nylon fishing line down the middle. Pull up tightly, and secure. Fluff net out into half circle. Repeat on rest of net. Place half circles back to back. Secure. Sew to back of t-shirt on one side of zipper. Hook other side. To hold tail against body, attach a cloth band inside shirt opposite tail and tie around the waist.

Hands:

Make mittens from socks, as described for squirrel.

Lay a piece of muslin across the top of actor's fingers and back of hand. Pad with layers of dacron, building up higher over fingers, tapering to back of hand. Lay a

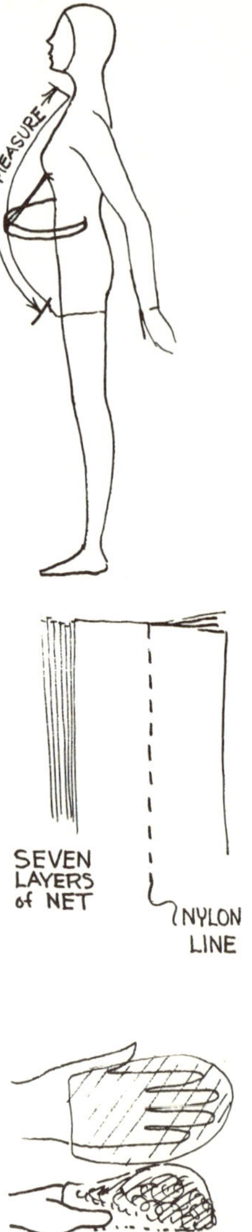

MAKE-UP FOR MRS. WARREN, A RABBIT

Mix	Effect Desired
1. No. 7 Brown No. 5L Ivory Yellow	Light Yellow Brown
2. White No. 5L Ivory Yellow A touch of No. 7	Light Tan. (Lighter than above Yellow Brown, but must contrast with White).
3. No. 7 Brown liner White	Medium Brown (Darker in value than Yellow Brown).
4. No. 2 Moist Rouge White	Medium Pink.

Procedure:

1. Using Medium Brown: outline all areas, including eyes.

2. Fill in White next to pupil area. Make White nose (Area A).

3. Light Tan: Fill in Area B.

4. Light Yellow Brown: Areas C, D, E.

5. Medium Brown: Areas F, G. H.

6. No. 25 Brown Liner: lines on eyes, forehead, chops, under chin, whisker dots.

7. Medium Pink: Nose and mouth, inner corner of eyes.

8. Black: pupils, nostrils.

9. After Powdering: if necessary glue cheek pads to face.

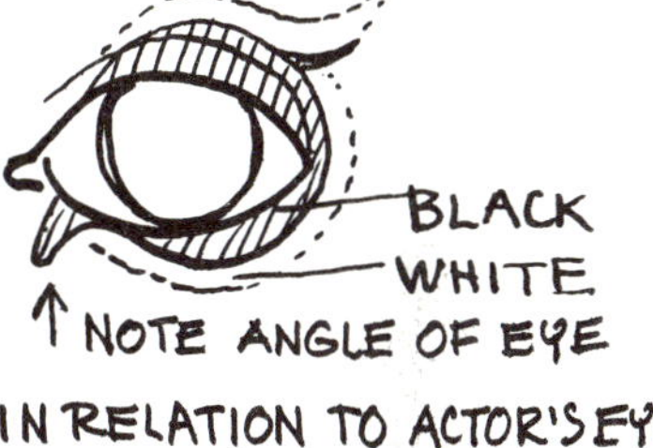

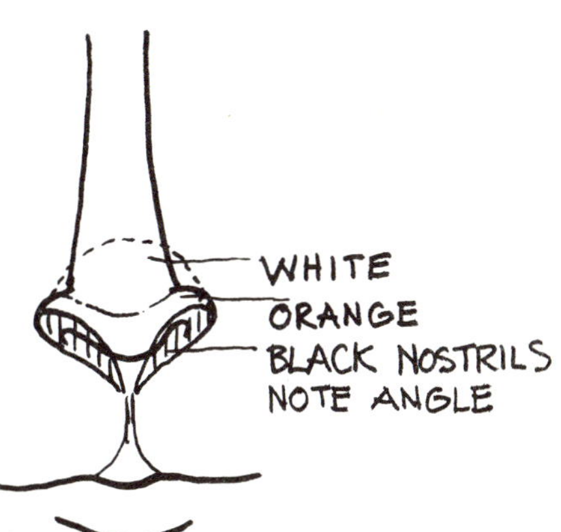

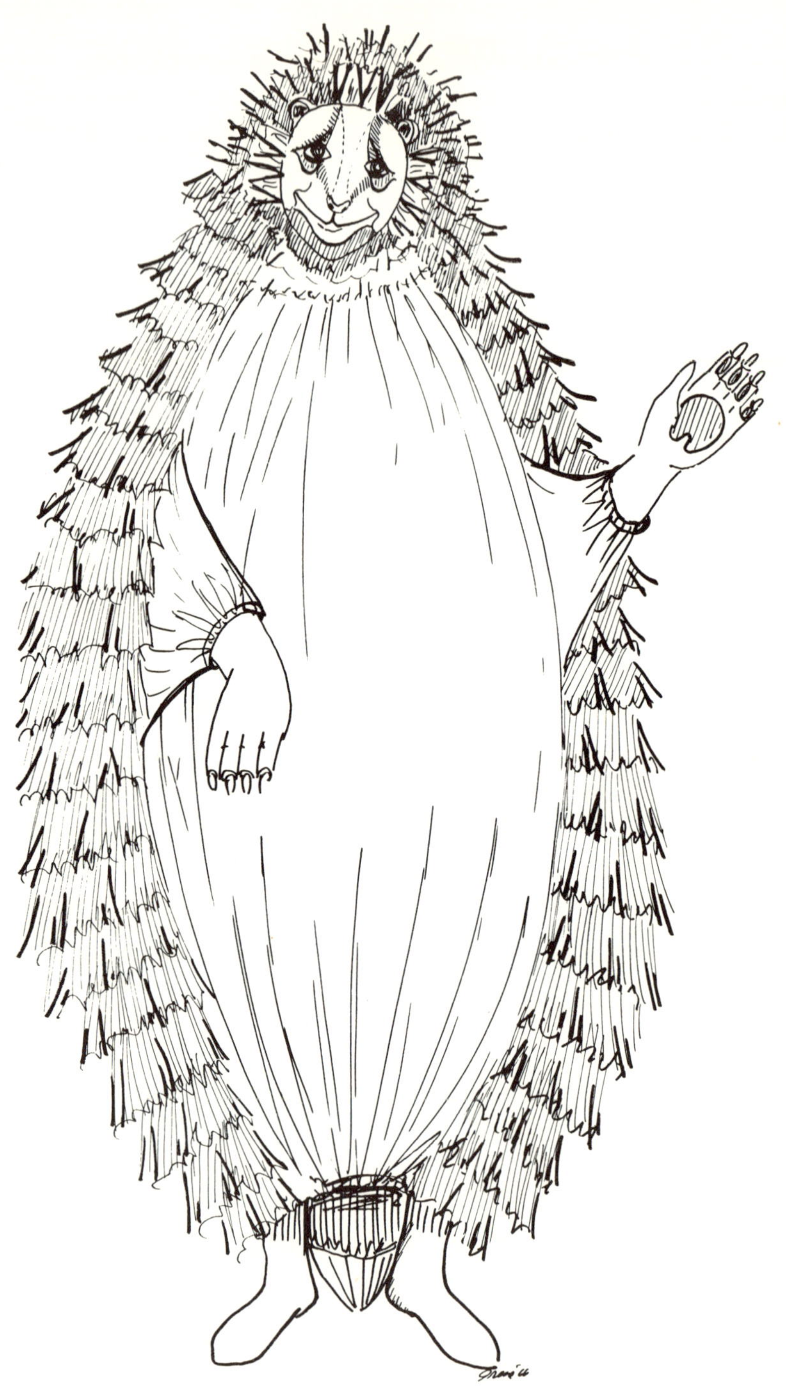

COSTUME FOR MR. SPINEY, A HEDGEHOG

Materials:

T-Shirt: grey

Tights: grey

Socks: grey

Gloves: grey, cotton work gloves

Fabrics: black cotton, for wimple, tail

black net, for "fur" on body and head

white net, around face. 1/4 yd.

black organdy, for body

light grey cotton, for under-belly, sleeves

grey felt; fingers, overgloves

pink felt, for ears

black felt, paw prints

White pipe cleaners: quills

Hoop wire

Twill tape

Elastic

Masking tape

Black felt marker

Desired Effect:

For all his prickly exterior the hedgehog has a few soft spots, as indicated by his wistful and somewhat pensive face. The shell of quills, expressed in organdy ruffles and prickly pipe cleaners, contrasts to a soft under-belly. As only small portions of the hands and legs extend beyond the cocoon of net, the short-legged appearance of the hedgehog is secured. He should appear to be a round mound of quills mounted on stubby legs. He rolls up in ball to sleep and has a generally good disposition. His nose is a snout like that of a pig.

Basic Garments:

The actor will wear a grey t-shirt, tights, socks over the tights, or grey soft shoes.

Body:

Hoops: Make a hoop of hoop wire which goes around the shoulder. Press it to body in front, and let it extend out from body 6 or 7 inches in the back. This hoop will overlap and hook at left front.

Make a second hoop at hip level, pressed against the body in front. Let it sag slightly in back. (A curve drawn from head to foot touching the hoops at center back should give a curve which is fuller at bottom.) Tape hoop together.

Make a waist band which has twill tape running to back and sides of large hoop. Fasten a band to hoop at center front and tie around hips.

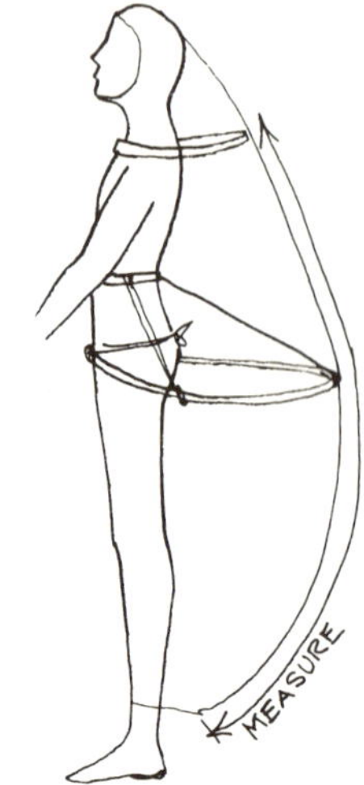

Measure from neck over hoops to ankles at center back. Cut two widths of black organdy this length. Measure side from neck over hoops to ankles. Using this measurement, cut one piece from light grey cloth, and one from black net. Handle as one piece of cloth to form the front panel.

Seam back panels together. Lay flat beside front panel, which will be shorter. Trim on a curve from center back to side front. Continue on front panel curving up to 10 inches at center front. Face edge to make casing for elastic.

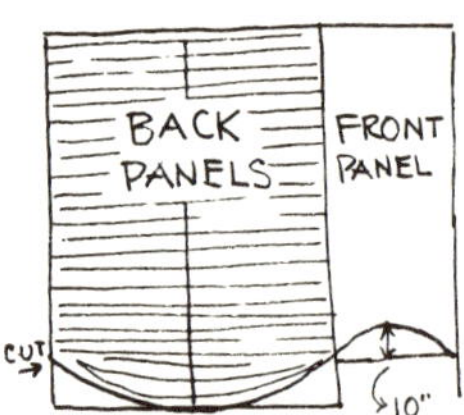

Chalk mark lines 2½ inches apart, easing into curve at bottom.

Cut black net strips across width of fabric, 6 inches wide. Gather down the center of two layers at a time. Fold on gathering line and stitch across gathers so that all four layers are under control.

Lay on marked lines, and at 3 or 4 inch intervals, sew in a white pipe cleaner folded in a "V." The pipe cleaners should be bent with ends uneven by about one-half inch. Sew sides to front panel, leaving 12 inch slit for arms, centered at elbow level.

From light grey cotton cut two rectangles 12 inches by 24 inches. Sew the 12 inch ends together. Turn under one half inch on one end of tube. Insert elastic to fit wrist. Sew other end into slit at side front. Repeat for other arm.

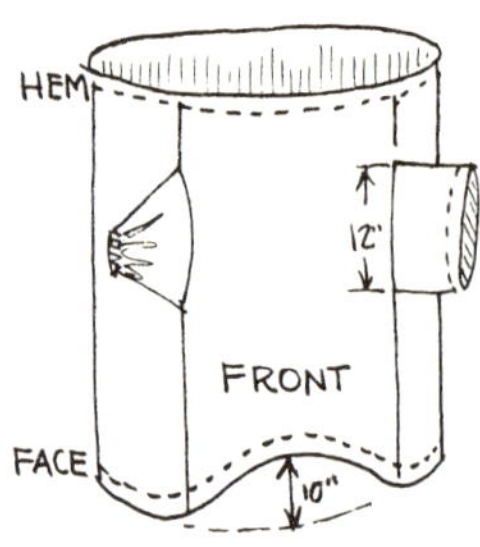

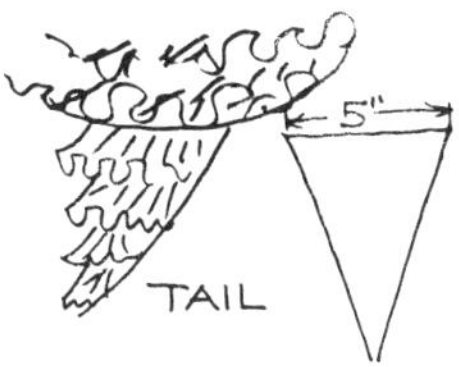

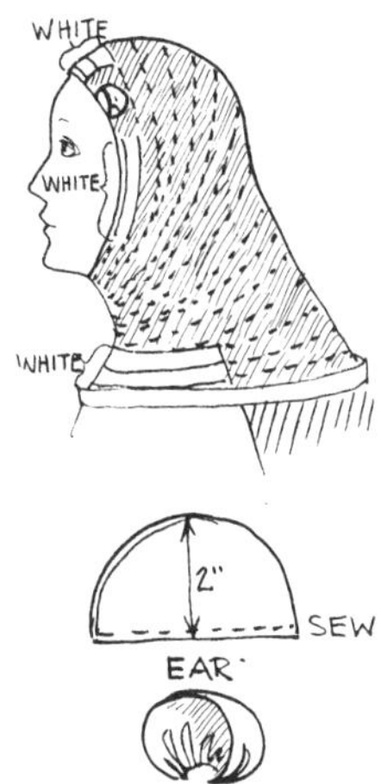

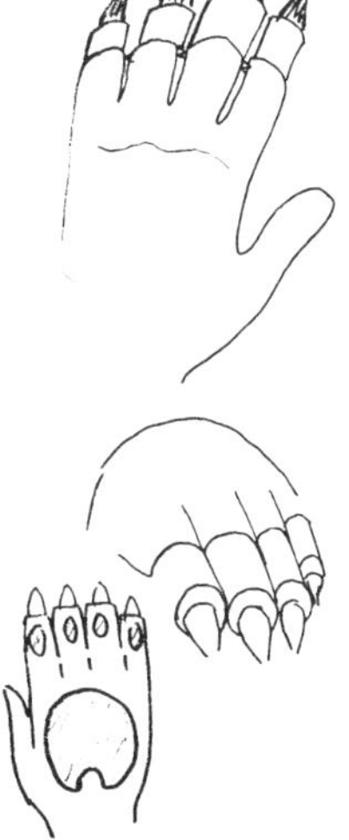

Hem top edge. Run elastic through to gather loosely about neck. Run elastic through casing at bottom.

Tail:

Cut a triangular piece of black cotton which will reach from center back of hoop to the floor, dragging slightly. Sew on rows of net ruffles, as above, eliminating pipe cleaners. Sew to hoop.

Head:

Cut a basic wimple from black cotton, except that about 6 inches down from the crown, start to taper out so that wimple will be full at shoulders. It should fit easily over the top shoulder hoop.

Ears:

Cut ears from pink felt and black organdy in a circle 4 inches in diameter. Cut in half. Sew layer of organdy and felt together on straight edge. Turn. Gather curved edge. Sew in cupped shape to wimple as shown in design on makeup chart.

Mark wimple for rows of ruffles. Place no more than 2 inches apart. Make net ruffles in the same way as those for body, but put pipe cleaners closer together on head: one inch apart on white net row, and 2 inches apart on black ruffles. They can become further apart toward shoulders.

Examine the makeup face of hedgehog to find areas where white meets the wimple. Mark these areas on forehead and at cheeks. The first two rows of net next to these areas will be white net. Sew white rows in place first, then black. No quills are used immediately under chin. The last few rows under the chin should be white to begin to blend with the lighter under-belly. Extend them out to the side to correspond to the sides of front panel on body.

Hands:

Use large cotton work gloves. To create the short, fat paws of the hedgehog, tack the gloves together at the middle knuckles. Wrap fingers of gloves in two or three layers of grey felt, to make them round and fat, beyond the middle knuckle. Leave the last joint of the finger sticking out. Wrap this in masking tape to make as pointed as possible. Paint tape black with felt marker. Cut paw prints from black felt and sew to palm of glove.

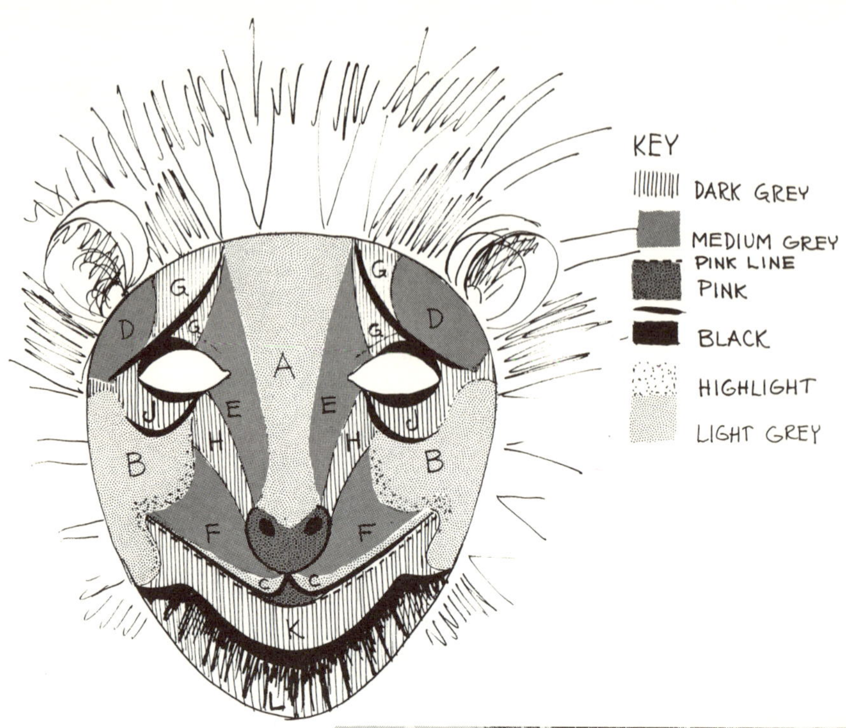

MR. SPINEY, A HEDGEHOG

Make-Up Supplies

Stein's Grease Stick:

No. 25 Black

No. 22 White

Moist Rouge:
No. 3 Medium Red

MAKE-UP FOR MR. SPINEY, A HEDGEHOG

Mix	Effect Desired
1. No. 22 White No. 25 Black	Light Grey
2. Same colors as above, with more Black.	Medium Grey
3. Same colors as above, with more Black.	Dark Grey
4. No. 3 Medium Moist Rouge No. 22 White	Medium Pink

Procedure:

1. Outline all areas.
2. Light Grey: areas A, B, C.
3. Medium Grey: areas D, E, F. Fade F into C.
4. Dark Grey: areas G, H, J, K, L.
5. Pink: Nose, mouth. Lightly stroke pink away from nose into Grey area A.
6. White: highlight along "laugh-line" of Area B.
7. Black: eyes, lines above and below eyes, nose, mouth, under chin. Brush in area under chin (area L) in strokes to resemble quills. Continue till it meets Wimple.

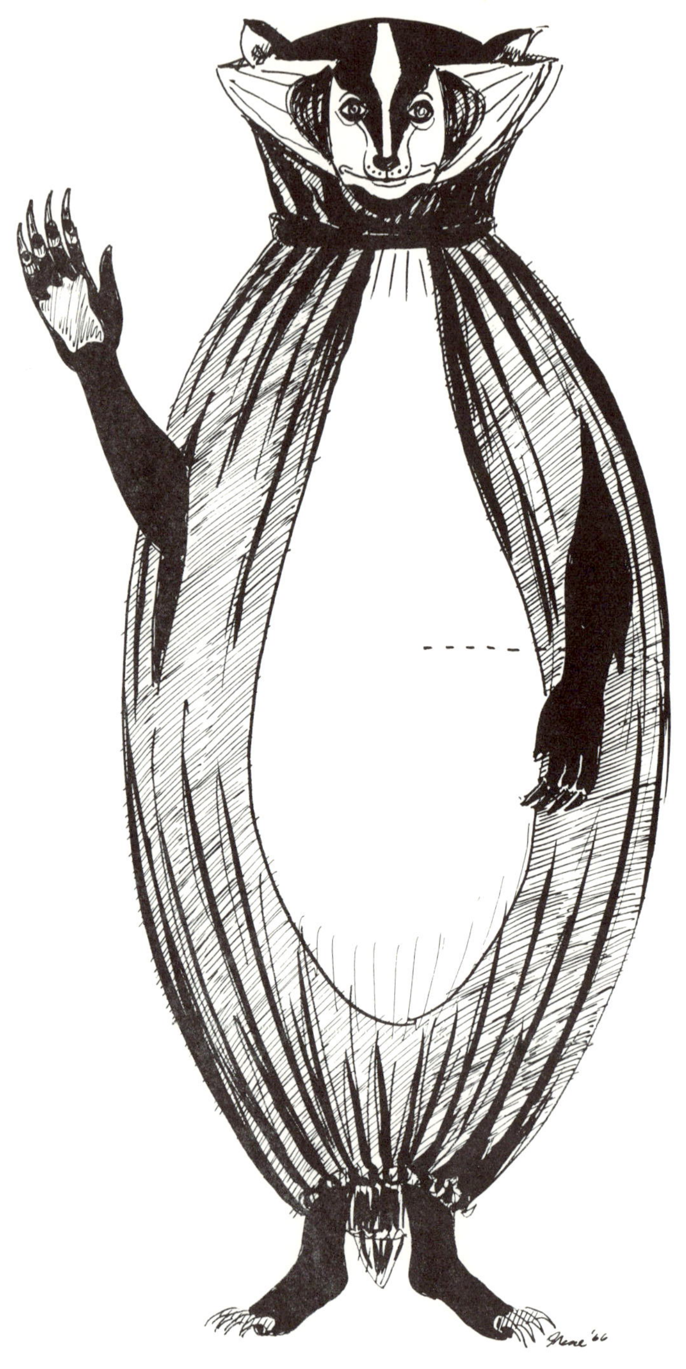

COSTUME FOR MR. SETT, A BADGER

Materials:

Tights and T-shirt: black

Gloves: black

Socks: black

Fabrics: White Organdy: under-belly, back stripe, cheeks, ears

Black Organdy: body, cheeks, ears

Black Cotton: wimple, tail

Black Net: body

Grey Felt: paw prints

Black plastic electrician's tape

Hoop wire

Plastic bottle (such as household bleach comes in)

Masking tape

Black Felt Marker

Black twill tape

Elastic

Desired Effect:

The badger is a rather rounded animal with short legs, and long
efficient claws with which to burrow. His head is broad, rounding
out into his body. By translating his rotundity into a cocoon of net
supported by hoops, his "fur" will swing and move lightly with his
body. Slits allow the arms to come through only up to the elbows,
giving the effect of short "paws." Elastic pulls the cocoon close about
the shins, showing short legs, and contributing to the short steps
needed by the actor to create the scurrying gait of the badger. Mr.
Sett is the master mind among his friends, generally leading and making decisions. His sharp black and white color scheme lends him
strength of character and dominance of the stage

Basic Garments:

Tights and T-shirt are worn with sleeves of shirt tucked into wrist of gloves. Gloves should have elastic sewed in wrist. Black socks are worn over the tights.

Hoops:

Create hoops from hoop wire in proportion to the figure. The first hoop is sewed to the side of wimple, horizontally, at forehead. Fasten to center back of wimple. Suspend on sides by piece of twill tape tacked on top of wimple.

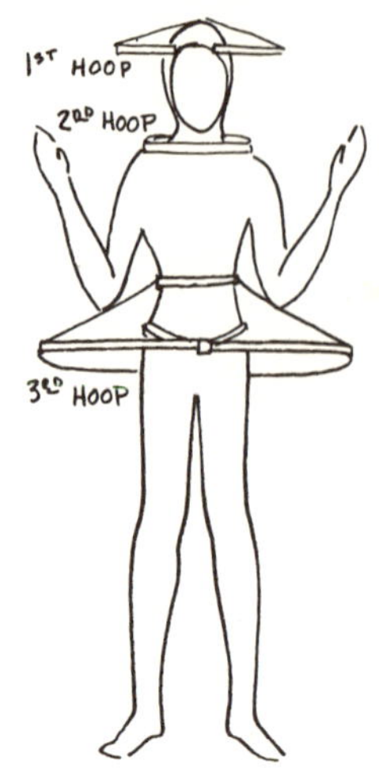

The second hoop rests on the shoulders, and is slightly less wide than the shoulders, hooping out further in back. It should overlap and hook on left side of the front at seam running from arm slit. Fasten a tape on side back which will hook to side of wimple.

The third hoop should be about twice as wide as the head, fastened together permanently with masking tape. It will be located about 6 inches below the waist, secured to the hips by means of a cloth band tied to center front of hoop, and then around the hips. Suspend the hoop from a band around the waist with twill tape running to the hoop on sides and to center back.

Body:

Measure shoulder to ankles, with hoops in place—allowing extra for pouf. It should measure longer in back because the hoop sticks out further there. Using this measurement, cut three panels from black net, and from black organdy. Cut out a curve on the bottom of the front panel, about 10 inches deep.

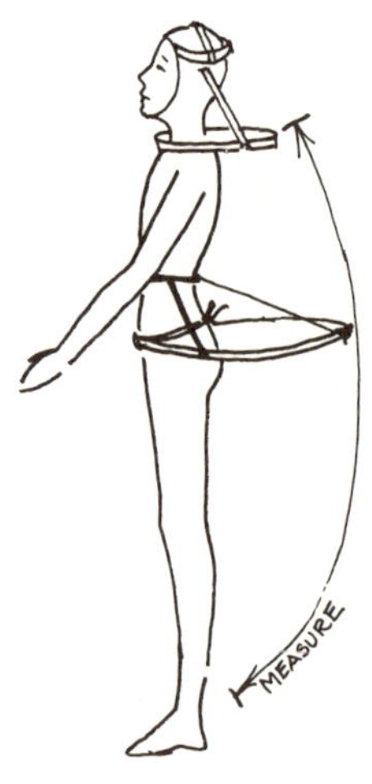

Cut from white organdy the shape for the under-belly. Sew to the front panel.

Sew panels together, leaving slits for arms on side front seams. Run gathering threads along top edge. Turn under one inch hem on bottom for elastic. Draw elastic in, using a piece about 24 inches long and ½ inch

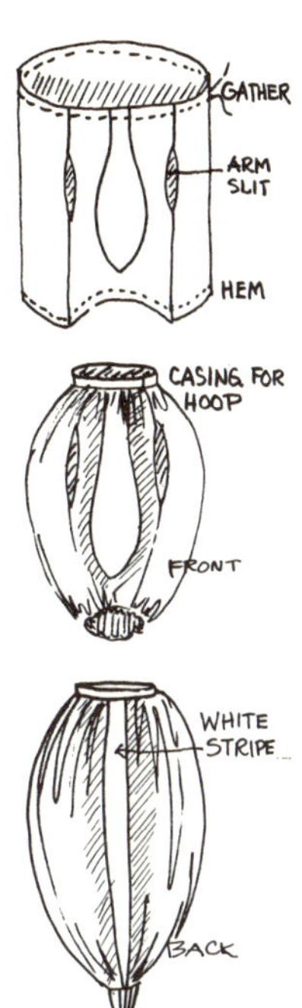

wide. Bind arm slits for strength. Finish seam, above left arm for hooks and eyes.

Adjust gathers at top to fit top hoop. Using a straight strip of black cotton, make a casing to receive hoop wire. Insert. Overlap ends of hoop so that it will retain its circular shape. Sew on large hook.

Cut a white organdy strip to run down back.

Tail:

Cut a triangular piece of black cotton about 4 inches wide, and long enough to touch the floor. Cut two half circles of black net the same radius as the depth of tail. Run gathering thread around outside edge. Sew sides of net to sides of tail. Sew cotton part of tail to center back of costume at bottom. Gather the net and pull the center up two inches higher than top of tail. Whip to costume. This will force the tail out at an angle, rather than hanging straight down.

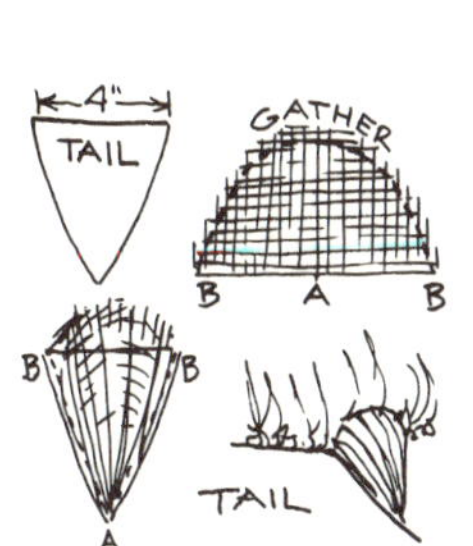

Hands:

Cut from side of plastic bleach bottle, triangular pieces for claws. They should be about two inches long, and wide enough at the base to reach around the finger in the glove, and overlap. Tape to the finger of the glove just above the middle knuckle, with black plastic electrician's tape. Make claws black with felt marker. The claws could also be made of Sculptofab or Celastic, which would allow the shaping of a downward curve.

Cut in the same way for the toes, slightly fitting over ends of toes through socks. Tape to form tubes. Heat a large needle or ice pick, and burn holes through the plastic so claws can be sewed to socks.

Cut paw prints from grey felt, and sew to palms of gloves.

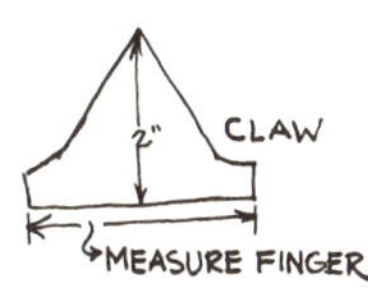

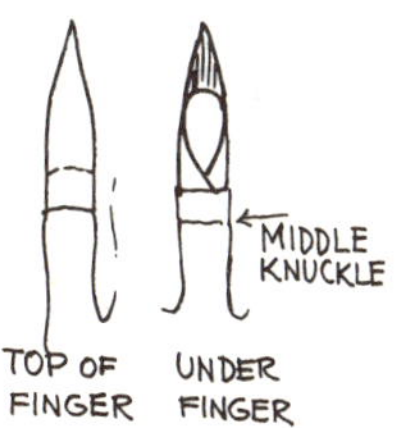

Head:

Cut basic wimple from black cotton. Fit closely about the face, particularly at forehead.

Cut a piece of hoop wire 32 inches long. Magic mark it black, or cover with black cloth. Sew ends to edge of wimple high on forehead. Ends will be about 4 inches apart across the forehead. Sew center back of hoop to wimple. Tie twill tape to sides and sew to crown of wimple.

Cut a double layer of black net, about 40 inches by 24 inches. Pin to wimple at center front, and pull back across the ears. Tack to wimple by ears. Gather end of net at shoulder level, stitch gathers to wimple, loosely, and trim off extra ends.

Lay an 18″ square of black organdy on the head, with the tip extending over the forehead. Smooth it over the hoop and down the back. Mark where it hits the hoop. Cut, turn under, and sew to top of hoop. Shape in back with large gathers. Tack in place over net gathers. At forehead edge, cut to shape, allowing seam. Sew to wimple.

Cheeks:

Cut a 10 inch circle from white organdy. Pleat from center, like a fan. Turn under pleats against face edge of wimple. Consult Makeup chart to see where white begins: about one-half inch below mouth, up to hoop. Tack to top of hoop, and to wimple by ear.

For black cheeks, cut a triangular piece of black organdy about the length of the white pleated area along the face line. Tuck under at cheeks, tack, and gather to bottom corner. Turn ends under, and tack. The way in which these gathers are made should create a curve on the outside. Trim with scissors, if necessary.

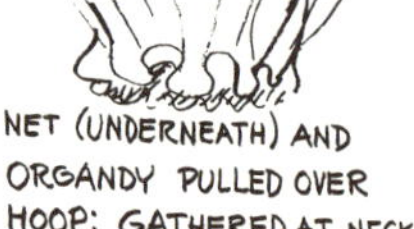

NET (UNDERNEATH) AND ORGANDY PULLED OVER HOOP; GATHERED AT NECK

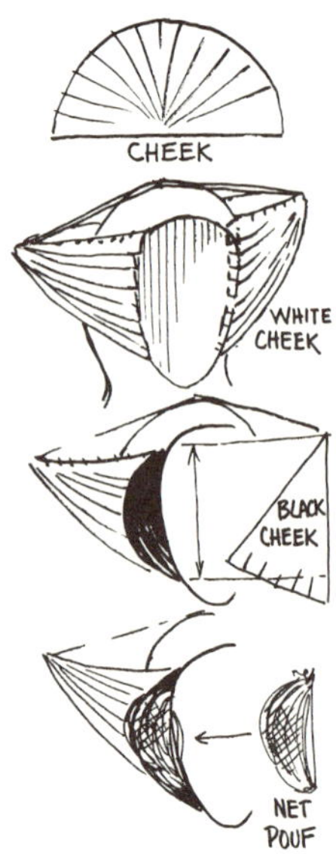

Cut two pieces of black net 8 inches by 12 inches. Gather loosely, by hand, across the narrow ends. Attach on top of black cheek, to give extra cheek pouf.

From white organdy cut center strip. Width at forehead will be approximately 1½ inches wide, getting wider as it goes back.

It should meet the stripe applied to the body at center back. At forehead, tuck stripe under wimple and tack.

Ears:

Cut 2 triangles each from black and white organdy. Stitch edge. Turn. Gather across bottom. Measure 3 inches from where hoop begins on forehead, outward, to locate ear. Shape bottom of ear into semi-circle, and pin so that point leans outward. Sew to hoop and organdy.

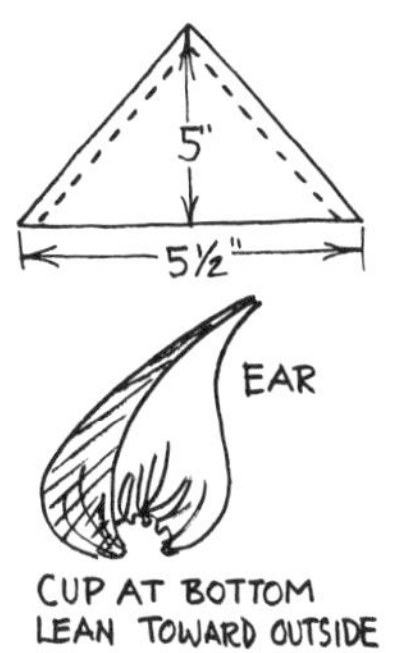

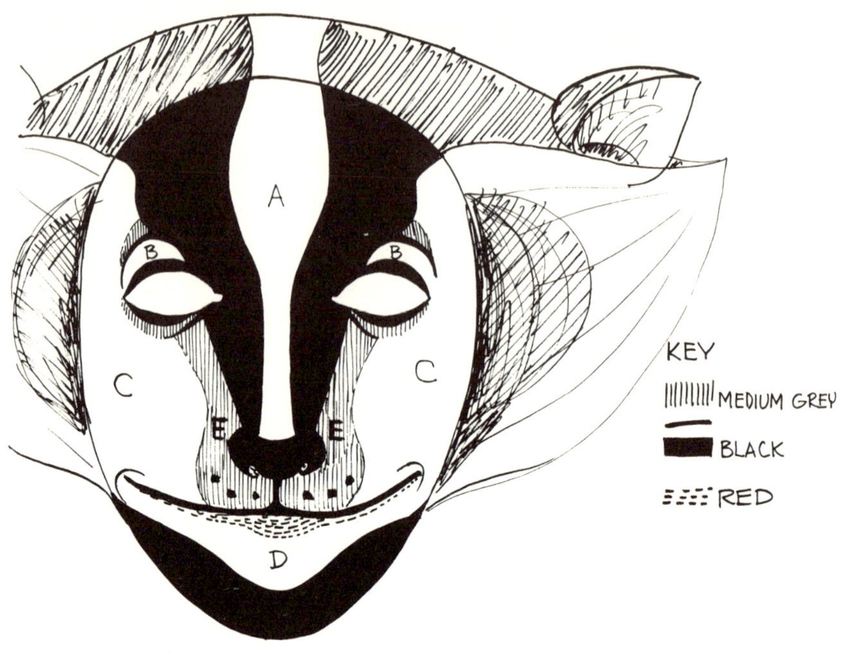

MR. SETT, A BADGER

Make-Up Supplies

Stein's Grease Stick:
   No. 25 Black
   No. 22 White

Moist Rouge:
   No. 3 Medium Red

MAKE-UP FOR MR. SETT, A BADGER

Mix	**Effect Desired**
No. 22 White	Medium Grey which contrasts well
No. 25 Black	with Black and White.

Procedure:

1. Outline all areas in medium Grey. Draw eyes first, then nose. Note position of the Badger's nose in relation to actor's nose.

2. White: areas A, B, C, D.

3. Medium Grey: area E.

4. Black: areas F, G, and nose. (H)

5. Black: Eyes, line above Badger's eyelids, whisker dots, mouth and chop line.

6. Medium Grey: shadow above eyelids, below eyes, laugh-lines at end of mouth.

7. Red: nostrils, mouth, below the black line.

Note: The white stripe on forehead should meet the stripe on the costume.

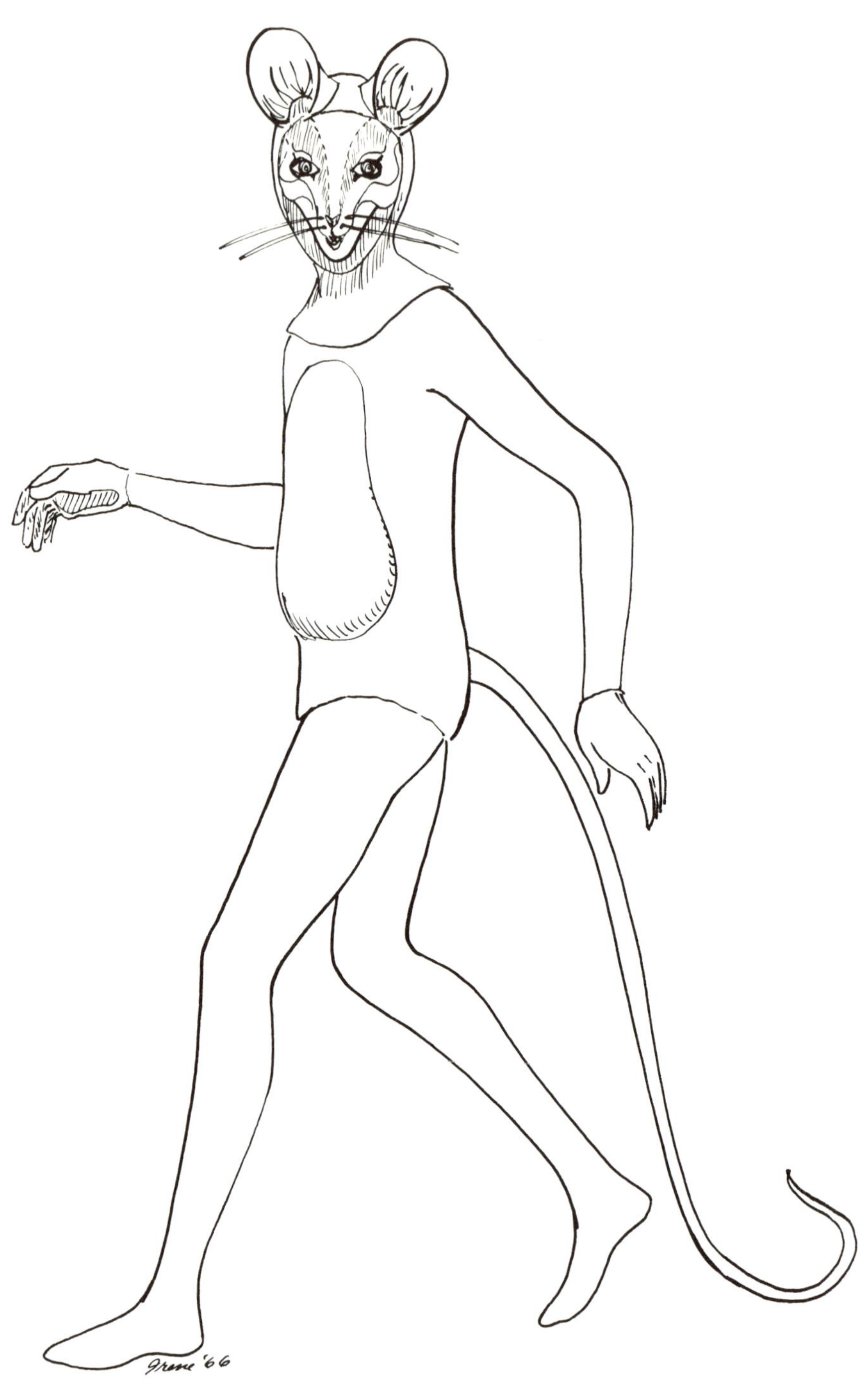

Grose '66

COSTUME FOR MR. PADDLE, A WATER RAT

Materials:

T-shirt: charcoal grey

Tights: charcoal grey

Socks: charcoal grey

Gloves: charcoal grey

Fabrics: charcoal grey cotton, wimple, tail
pink organdy, ears, under-belly, pads
grey organdy, ears
black organdy, 2 one inch bias strips

Millinery wire

Hoop wire

Dacron batting

Elastic

Black garter belt with hook fastening

Button thread.

Aluminum clothes-line wire

Desired Effect:

Mr. Paddle is not a particularly offensive rat—in fact he seems
quite harmless, as the touches of pink might indicate. His well filled
costume gives his body a neat appearance, with ears and tail as accent.
The tail does little except drag, but such large ears are made to hear
with. These ears combined with the button-eyed, sharp-whiskered
face, should catch all noises with concentrated intensity.

Basic Garments:

T-shirt, charcoal grey, should be somewhat fitted. Wear sleeves tucked into gloves at wrist. Wear grey socks over feet of tights, or ballet shoes.

Body:

Put t-shirt on actor. Draw shape of under-belly. Pad with dacron, making it slightly fatter on stomach. Cut pink organdy on bias to cover dacron. Turn under edges. Sew to shirt.

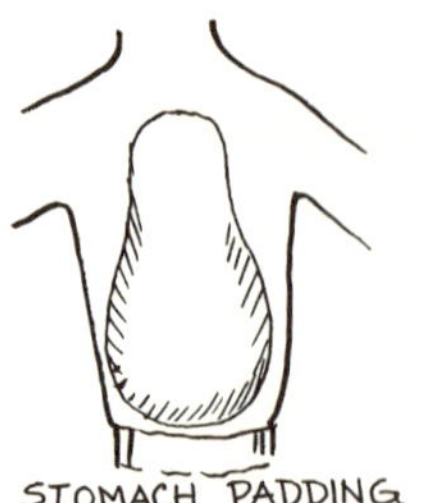

Tail:

Bend aluminum clothes line into spiral, which will fit flat against the actor's back. Bend away at right angle. Curve down slightly. Let wire extend 10 inches from body.

Cut a bias strip of grey cotton that will reach from actor's back, along tail wire, and drag the floor about 12 inches. Lay a strip of hoop wire the length of cotton. Lay a roll of dacron in center, on top of the wire. Pull edges up and overlap. Pin and sew. Slip onto tail wire. Sew end of hoop wire, and tail to garter belt.

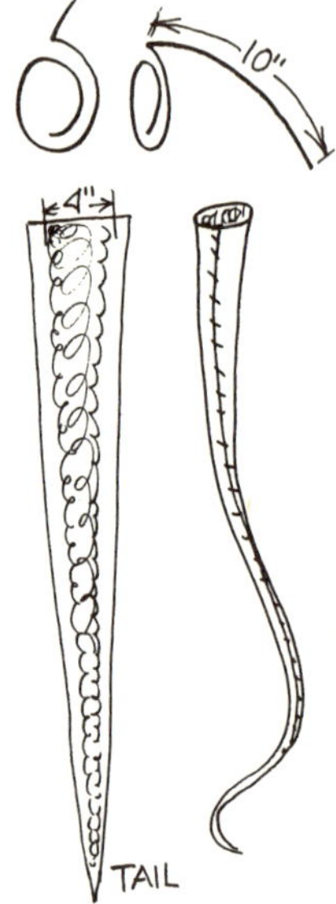

Tail Exit:

Fit t-shirt on actor. Mark where tail should come through. Sew facing around hole. Clip and turn.

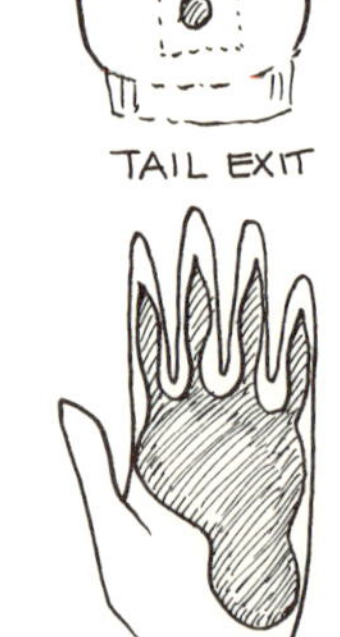

Hands:

Put elastic in wrist of glove. Tuck sleeves under gloves. Cut pink organdy (or felt) pads. Applique to palms of gloves.

Head:

Cut basic wimple from grey cotton. Take tucks to fit around neck.

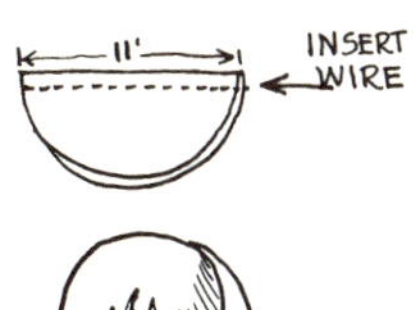

Ears:

For ears, cut two circles, 11 inches in diameter, one from pink and one from grey organdy. Cut circles in Half. Sew together along straight edge. Turn. Top stitch ¼ inch from edge. Gather rounded edge. Run millinery wire through straight edge. Shape into circular cup at bottom. Check design for placement. Sew to wimple.

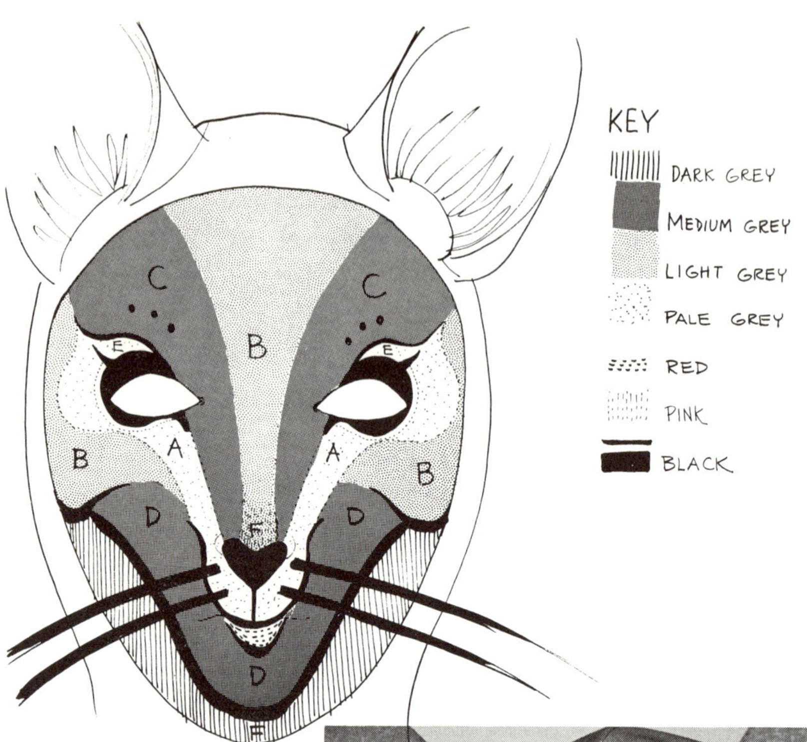

MR. PADDLE,
A WATER RAT

Make-Up Supplies

Stein's Grease Stick:

  No. 25 Black

  No. 22 White

Moist Rouge:

  No. 3 Medium Red

Spirit Gum

4 whiskers of rolled

  organdy

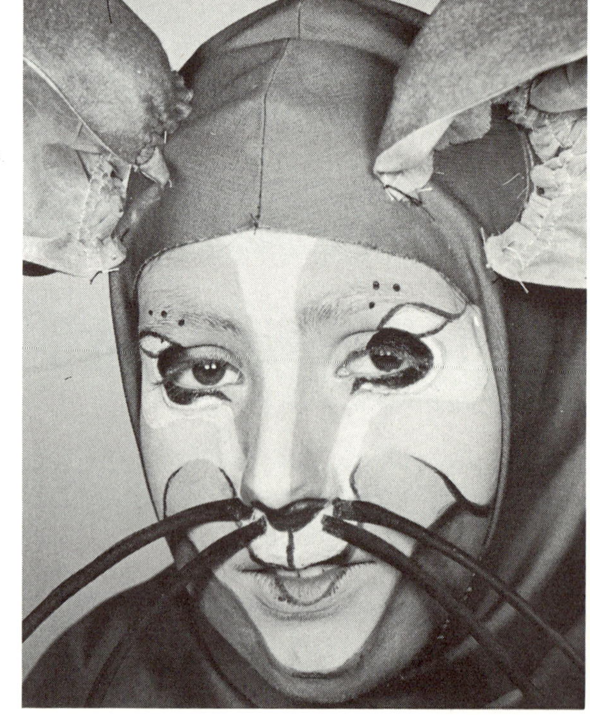

100

MAKE-UP FOR MR. PADDLE, A WATER RAT

Mix	Effect Desired
1. No. 22 White No. 25 Black	Very pale Grey (but dark enough to contrast to white).
2. Same	Light Grey.
3. Same	Medium Grey.
4. Same	Dark Grey. Test in strokes on back of hand to see that shades separate from each other in progressive steps.
5. White No. 3 Moist Rouge	Pale Pink, same value as light Grey.

Procedure:

1. Mix four shades of Grey varying in value from pale Grey to light Grey, medium Grey, and dark Grey.

2. Draw in basic lines and areas with Medium Grey. Start by drawing the eyes, noting the shape of the pupil in relation to actual eyes. When you look straight into the mirror the pupils should form a perfect circle around the outside edge of your eye. Next, locate the Rat's nose, which is below yours, on the area above your lip. All area lines swing out from the nose.

   Hold design beside your face and compare layout in mirror. Make all corrections now.

3. Draw White around pupil.

4. Fill in Black pupil.

5. Fill in Areas A and E with pale Grey.

6. Fill in Area B with light Grey.

7. Fill in Areas C and D with medium Grey.

8. Fill in Area F with dark Grey.

9. Black: paint nose tip.

10. Paint Pink next to nose, and shade upward into Grey.

11. Red on mouth (lower lip of actor) and at down corners of eyes.

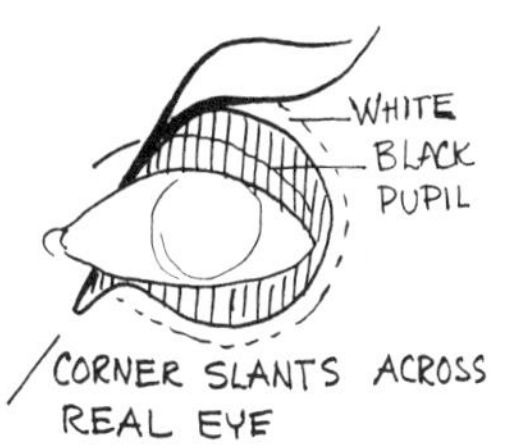

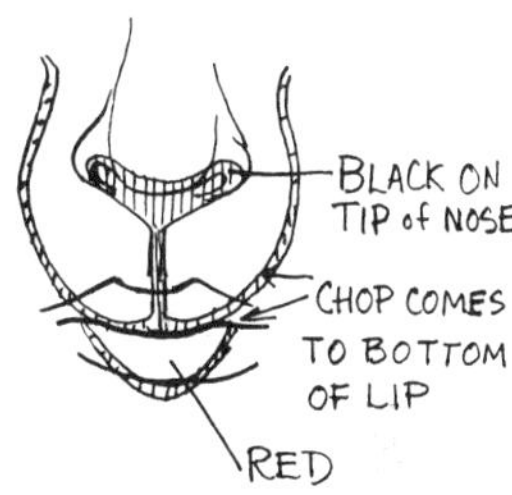

12. Draw on all Black lines: mouth and chops, over eyes, under chin.

13. Powder. Brush.

14. Glue on whiskers with spirit gum. Apply gum to face and whiskers; let dry, give second coat. Apply when tacky, horizontally with floor.

    Whiskers: Cut bias strips of Black organdy 1″ x 6″ long. Place on a taut fabric surface, like cloth-covered ironing board. Roll from edge with finger tips. Keep rolling until it forms a tight roll about the size of vermicelli.

COSTUME FOR MR. BRUSH, A SQUIRREL

Materials:

T-shirt: red-brown

Tights: red-brown

Socks or ballet type shoes: red-brown

Socks: red-brown, for mittens

Fabrics: red-brown cotton, for wimple
red-brown organdy, for tail
gold organdy, for tail

Plastic foam (the resilient type used in cushions)

Aluminum clothes line wire

Black garter belt, with hook fastening

Dacron batting

Button thread

Millinery wire

Elastic

Desired Effect:

The squirrel is a master of the sharp eye and quick movements. He is given a neat body, accented by nut-pouchy cheeks, and dominated by a glorious tail. The actor will not have the control of his tail that his teacher, the squirrel, does, but by practicing the sharp, quick, abrupt movements, he will achieve a similar effect.

Basic Garments:

If the tights, t-shirt, socks, cotton for wimple, and organdy are all bought in white, they can be dyed red-brown together to achieve a unity in color. The nylon tights dye quickly, and should be removed first.

Hands:

Dye a pair of large, men's, white cotton socks medium red-brown. Lay hand on sock, with fingers touching toe. Mark where wrist comes. Cut piece for thumb from corner of heel. Slit hand piece on one side. Sew in thumb. Use top of sock as cuff of mitten, using the elastic at the wrist. Cut paw prints from black felt and stitch to palm of mitten.

Tail:

Bend aluminum clothes line into flat spiral. This will fit flat against the body, just below the waist at center back. Bend out at a right angle from body. Curve out and up to one foot above the head. At end of curve, bend and return wire along same curve, repeating spiral at body.

Cut the suspenders from the garter belt. Use the hook fastening in the front. At center back, sew spiral to garter belt with button thread.

Measure tail wire. Cut long bias triangular piece out of brown organdy. Lay on it a tapering roll of dacron batting. Pull edges to center. Overlap, pin, and sew. Slide over tail wire. Sew base of tail to garter belt.

Cut strips of organdy: brown, 12 inches wide; gold, 14 inches wide. Working on four layers at one time, run heavy gathering thread down center by hand. Lay flat. Cut toward gathering thread, making fringe one-half inch wide. Gather. Sew to tail in a spiral, keeping rows about one inch apart. Start at tip of tail.

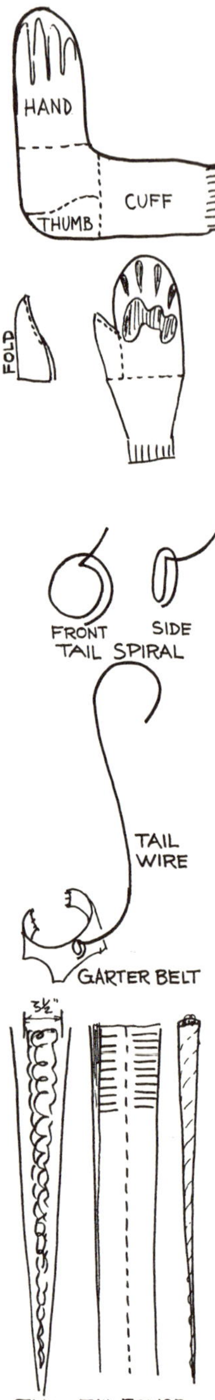

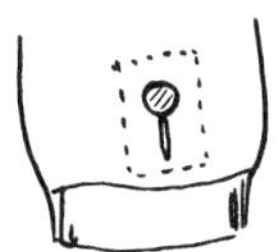

Tail Exit:

Put t-shirt and tail on actor. Mark where tail should come through shirt. Cut hole, and slit below it about 4 inches. Sew on facing, turn. Hook below hole.

The tail is mounted rather high toward the waist, so tights can ride beneath tail. If this seems uncomfortable, a tail exit can be made in tights.

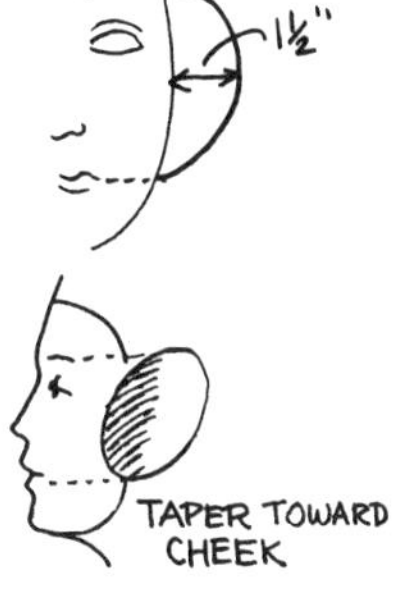

Head:

Cut basic wimple from red-brown cotton. Take darts at side of neck to make a neat fitting wimple.

Cheeks:

Study makeup design. Notice size of cheeks: height is from mouth to eyebrow, and cheek pad will be about 1½ inches thick. With scissors, snip off pieces of plastic foam until a half round shape is formed. The shape should taper in thickness, thinner as it reaches the cheek. Sew to wimple with about 1½ inches extending onto cheek.

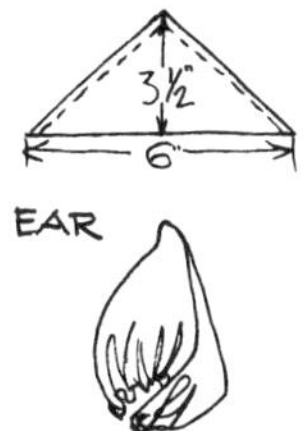

Ears:

Cut two ear triangles from brown organdy, and from gold organdy. Sew two thicknesses together, turn, top stitch ¼ inch from edge. Run gathering thread across bottom. Insert millinery wire on sides. Cup into round curve at bottom. Consult makeup design for placement. Sew to wimple.

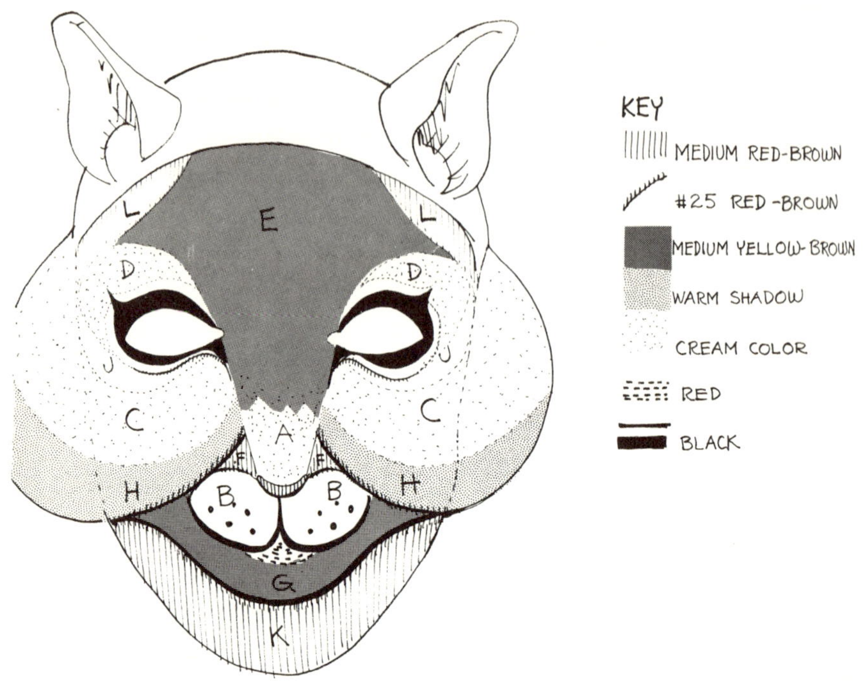

MR. BRUSH,
A SQUIRREL

Make-Up Supplies

Stein's Grease Stick:
    No. 5L Ivory Yellow
    No. 22 White
    No. 8 Dark Sunburn

Stein's Liner Stick:
    No. 25 Red Brown
    No. 16 Yellow
    No. 17 Black

Moist Rouge:
    No. 3 Medium Red

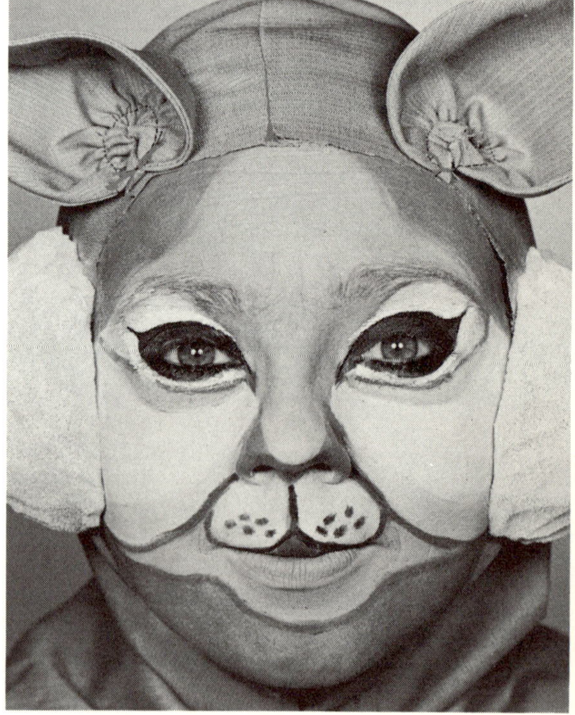

MAKE-UP FOR MR. BRUSH, A SQUIRREL

Mix	Effect Desired
1. No. 25 Red Brown liner No. 5L Ivory Yellow	Medium Yellow Brown
2. No. 25 Red-Brown liner White	Medium Red-Brown (darker than the above Yellow Brown)
3. No. 5L Ivory Yellow White	Cream Color
4. No. 5L Ivory Yellow No. 16 Yellow A touch of No. 8 Sunburn	Warm Shadow (Yellow Ochre)

Procedure:

1. Using medium Yellow - Brown, outline all areas including mouth and eyes on face. Begin with eyes, then mouth. Relate other areas to these.
2. Black: Fill in eyes. Black will cover whole eyelid. Must form circle on outside of eye, as actor looks straight into mirror.
3. Fill in white around pupil area.
4. Using Cream Color fill in areas A, B, C, D. Continue over cheek-pads with make-up. Area A fades up into area E (Area C continues out onto cheek pad.)
5. Use Medium Yellow - Brown: Fill Areas E, G. Fade Area E into Area A.
6. Use Yellow shadow color. Fill in Areas H, J. (Continue area H over Cheek-pads.)
7. Use Medium Red-Brown: Areas F, K, L.
8. Black: Draw mouth and chop line, whisker dots.
9. No. 25 Brown: nose, lines under chin, around cheeks, under eyes.
10. Red: Mouth, inner corners of eyes.
11. Put on Wimple. Continue areas C and H onto sponge cheeks with same colors. Powder. Glue foam cheeks to face if necessary.

Greene '66

COSTUME FOR MRS. DARK, A ROOK

Materials:

    T-shirt: black, long sleeved
    Tights: black
    Gloves: black
    Socks: grey
    Fabrics: black cotton, wimple, tail, chest
              black net, wings
              black silk organza, wings
              black satin, feathers
              blue and green satin, feathers

Dacron batting
Plastic coated work gloves, grey
Black garter belt, hook fastening
Aluminum wire
Hoop wire
Elastic

Desired Effect:

Mrs. Dark is a rather cold, arrogant character, who seems to be
a bit superior to her companions. Her grey and black color scheme
should augment this isolated superiority. The bird-like characteristics are captured in the costume by the padded breast and extended
tail. However, if the actress does not personally observe bird movements, she will never achieve the fast oscillation of the head which
makes the satin feathers shimmer; the hopping prance, exaggerated
by the large toes; or the impatient "wha," like a coarse "caw" which
causes the make-up beak to grow before our eyes.

Basic Garments:

A black cotton t-shirt, black tights, and black gloves with elastic sewed in wrists form the basic costume.

Body:

Chest Padding: Lay a piece of black cotton on the chest of the actor, over the t-shirt. Place dacron batting on top, in layers, slowly forming the desired shape. Taper to normal chest level at the edges. Lay another piece of black material on top of the dacron, pinning in dart where necessary to conform to the shape of the dacron. Trim off excess fabric at edges. After edges of padding are hemmed, the chest can either be whipped loosely to shirt, or attached all the way around with velcro fastener. T h e latter method allows easier washing of shirt.

On inside of shirt, at base of the center front of padding, sew cloth belt. Tie around waist to hold padding against body.

Cover whole chest with feathers, as described under instructions for head.

Tail Padding: Cover the seat of the actor, over the tights, with a square of black cotton, with the bias running up and down. Stretch to fit over the hips. Build out the tail pad with dacron batting, as on the chest. Check with the costume sketch for the silhouette desired. Another bias strip should be pinned to the under part of the pad, forming a "sling" to hold the padding. Pull the bias strip over the dacron, tacking edges in place. Tack the whole thing to the tights.

Tail Feathers:

Form a frame of aluminum wire across top of tail padding, and down, following the slope of the padding. Sew with button thread to top of padding and to elastic band of tights. Sew a garter belt to center back, (hooking in front), to help support weight and pull of tail. Cut suspenders off garter belt. Cover wire frame with black satin.

Cut eight pieces of black satin 4 inches by 24 inches with pinking shears. Through two

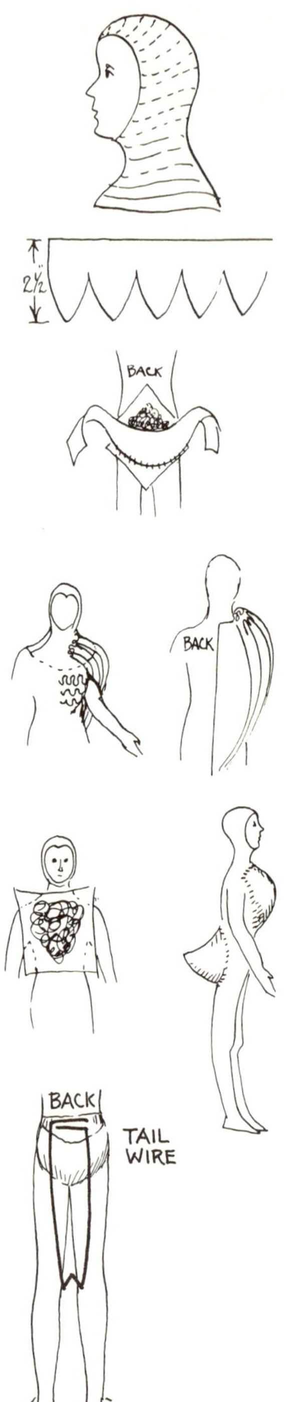

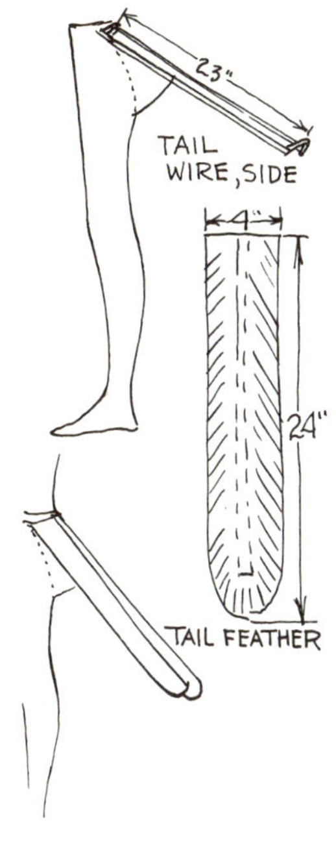

layers, stitch two rows down center to form casing for hoop wire. Machine stitch outer edge. Run hoop wire in casing. Secure ends of wire. Slash feathers on angle up sides.

Overlap two feathers on each side of wire frame. Fasten to frame as far down as end of tail padding.

Wings:

Using black net and black silk organza as one piece of fabric, cut a width long enough to reach from under the neck in front of the shoulder in a loose drape, to the point of the tail. Start draping one side at center back, leaving it smooth across the back, and gathering as you reach the shoulder and go over the arm around to side front. Pull the center back area taut to the tip of the tail, and loosely drape the gathered portion over the top of the arm, pulling it back to the tip of the tail. At the tail overlap the fullness into large flat pleats. Criss cross these at center back, forming an "X." Bind neck edge, and tie, or hook, in the front.

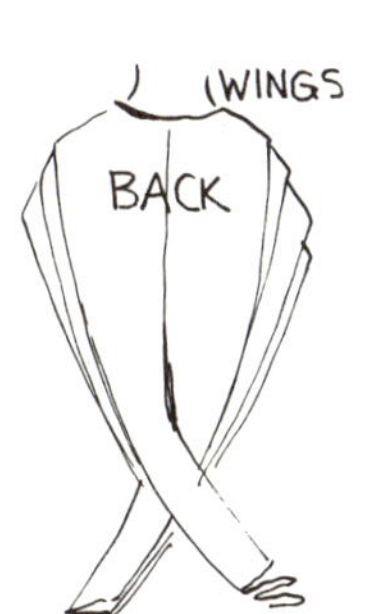

Head:

Cut a basic wimple from black cotton. Take darts on either side of the neck, for a neat fit.

Cut black satin (and a few strips of blue and green satin) into strips 2½ x 36 inches long. Scallop into feather shapes up to ½ inch from the top. Sew, or glue (Elmer's) on the wimple in single thicknesses, starting at the bottom, and working to the top, until the entire wimple is covered. Allow each layer to overlap slightly. Intersperse the blue and green feathers occasionally.

Feet:

Using grey plastic coated working gloves, cut hand off just above the thumb. Slip over the toe of the grey sock. Pull the sides and top to spread the fingers, which have now become toes. If the gloves are not stiff enough, stuff the fingers with dacron. Sew to sock. Sew thumb to back of sock for spur. Add extra elastic to top of sock.

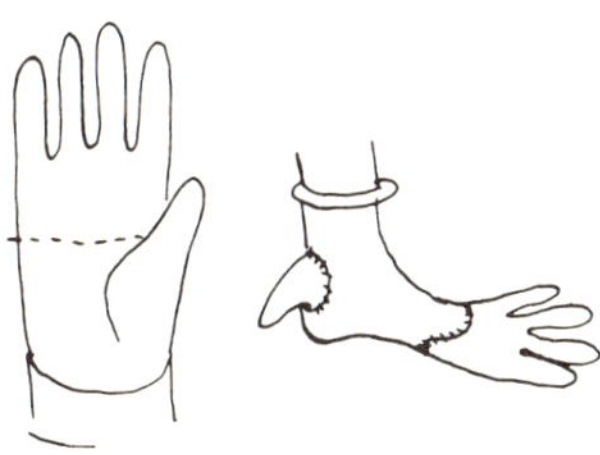

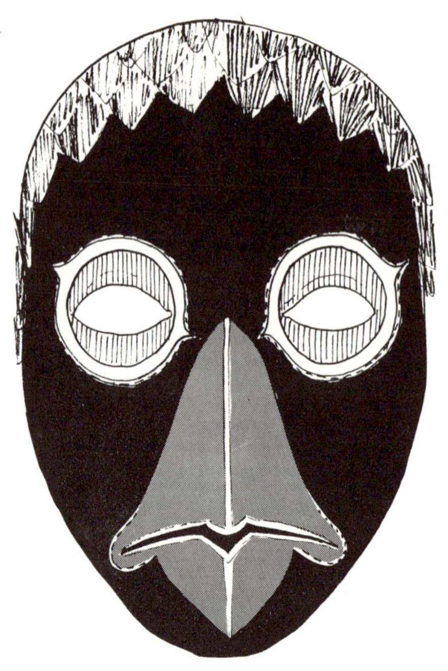

MRS. DARK, A ROOK

Make-Up Supplies

Stein's Grease Stick:
  No. 25 Black
  No. 22 White

Stein's Liner Stick
  No. 7 Brown

Moist Rouge:
  No. 3 Medium Red

Liquid Black tooth wax

Optional: Liquid Red

Alcohol: to remove tooth
wax

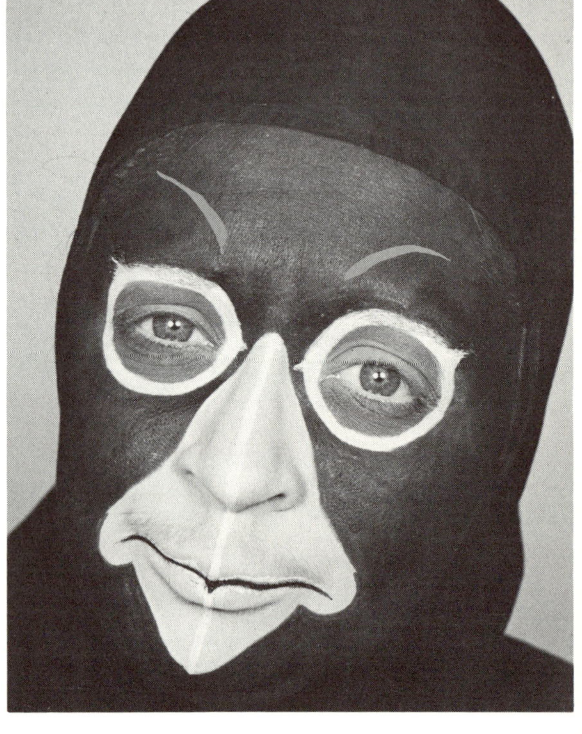

MAKE-UP FOR MRS. DARK, A ROOK

Mix	**Effect Desired**
No. 22 White No. 25 Black	Medium Grey which will sharply contrast with both black and white.

Procedure:

1. White: Outline all areas. Diameter of circle for eyes is determined by starting the circle at the corners of actual eye.

2. Fill in white circle around eyes. Draw white line down center of beak.

3. Fill in grey beak, area A.

4. Black: Draw black line of beak over actual mouth, forming point of beak on lower lip.

5. No. 7 Brown: Fill in eye. (Areas B inside white circles).

6. Outline Beak in white. (This step can be done after powdering to get a clearer line).

7. Red: Thin line around corners of mouth and around the eyes.

8. Fill in rest of face Black.

9. After powdering draw on eyebrow lines with white.

10. If desired, red line around eye may be applied with liquid red make-up.

11. Black out upper teeth with liquid black tooth-wax.

COSTUME FOR MR. BASKET, A DOG

Materials:

T-shirt: large size, red-brown

Tights: red-brown

Socks: red-brown, two pair

Fabrics: red-brown cotton, for wimple and tail   ,
red-brown velvet, or velveteen (or cotton), for ears
dark, red-brown cotton, for spots
black felt, for pads

Millinery wire

Aluminum wire

Button thread

Elmer's glue

Black garter belt, hook fastening

2 lead weights

Desired Effect:

By means of long floppy ears, wagging tail, big feet and a bumptious, boisterous gait, our dog will give that amiable "willing-to-please" quality necessary for Mr. Basket. The "look of concern" adds to this quality of serious service.

Basic Garments:

T-shirt, tights, socks, and cotton fabric for wimple and tail, could be purchased white, and dyed reddish-brown in one batch. Remove tights first, as nylon dyes quickly.

Body:

Spots: Cut spots from dark, red-brown cotton. Glue to shirt on back and on back of sleeves. Apply glue right next to raw edge of spots, and it will not ravel. Elmer's glue will dry clean, but will not wash. Spot back of wimple, also.

Tail: Form tail spiral from aluminum wire to fit flat against back. Bend away from body in right angles, and upward 6 inches. Cut millinery wire 24 inches long. Bend along same spiral as aluminum wire, but allow it to extend beyond in a curve measuring 20″ from back to tip.

Cut a bias triangle of red-brown cotton 21 inches long. Lay a roll of dacron in center. Fold edges up and overlap. Sew. Slide over tail wire. Tape wires together so they will slip in. Sew to garter belt with button thread. Hook belt in front. Cut suspenders off belt.

Tail Exit: Fit tail and shirt on actor. Mark hole where tail should come through. Sew facing to the hole, cut, and turn facing inside.

Hands:

Use two pairs of large men's cloth socks, dyed red-brown. Proceed according to directions given under the RABBIT. Cut pads from black felt and sew to palms of mittens.

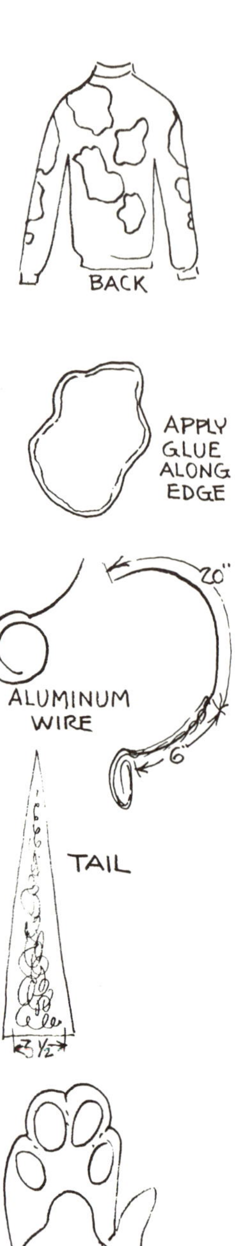

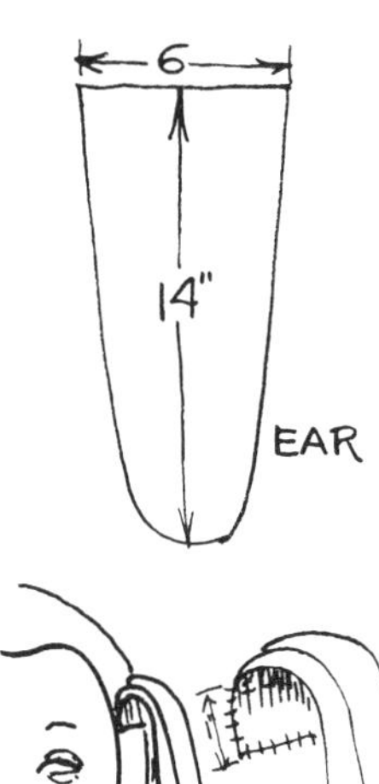

Feet:

Use other pair of red-brown socks, and follow directions given under the RABBIT.

Head:

Cut a basic wimple from red-brown cotton, taking two darts on either side of the neck to make a neat fit. Note the line of cut at the forehead of wimple.

Ears:

Make ear pattern, and cut four pieces from brown velvet or velveteen, if possible. If not, dark, red-brown cotton will serve. Sew edges and turn. Insert and sew lead weight in bottom of ear. Pleat to 3 inches across the top. Study design to locate placement of ears. Point pleated edge down, and sew up one inch on sides, and across.

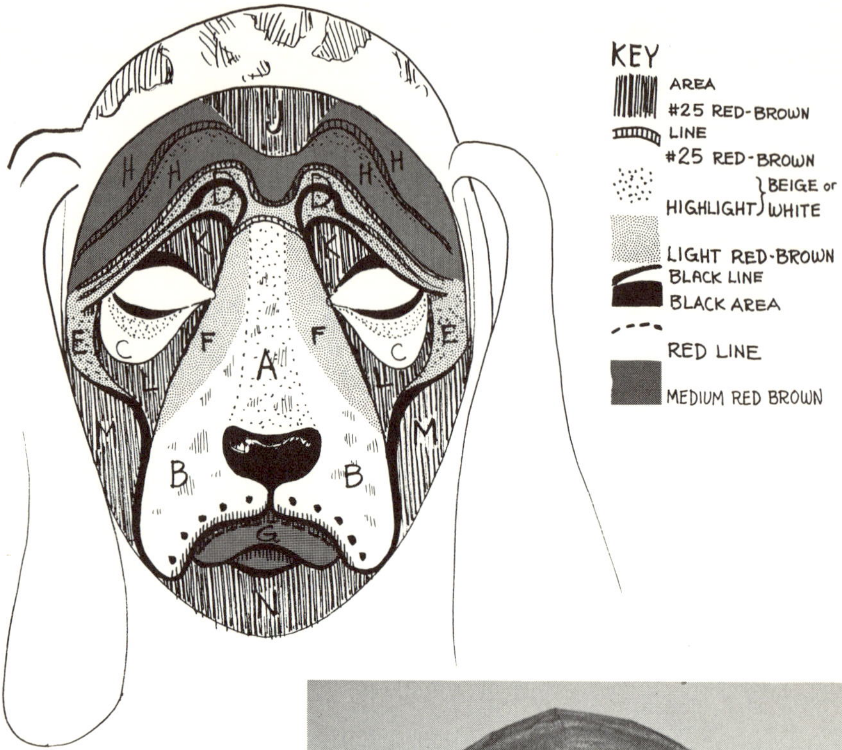

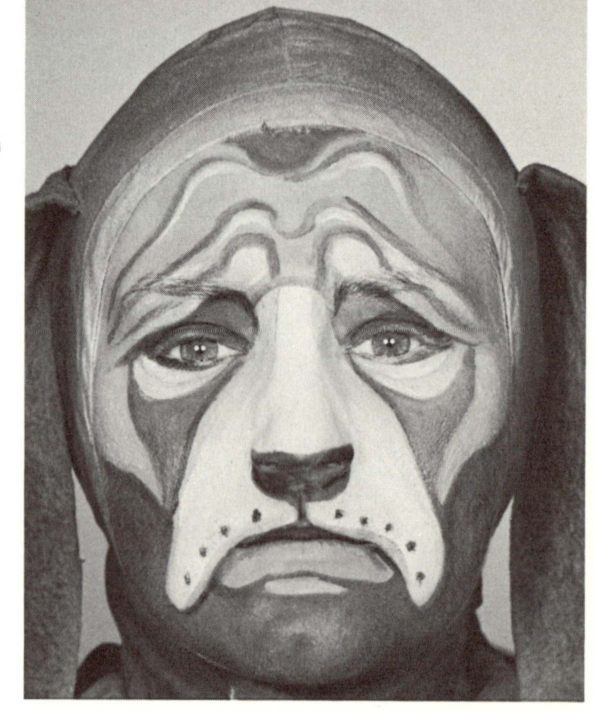

MR. BASKET, A DOG

Make-Up Supplies

Stein's Grease Stick:

No. 8 Dark Sunburn
No. 22 White
No. 5L Ivory Yellow

Stein's Liner Stick:

No. 17 Black
No. 25 Red-Brown

Moist Rouge:
No. 3 Medium Red

MAKE-UP FOR MR. BASKET, A DOG

Mix	**Effect Desired**
1. No. 22 White No. 8 Dark Sunburn A touch of No. 25 Brown liner	Medium Reddish Brown.
2. Same colors as above plus white	Light Reddish Brown.
3. Same colors as above plus white	Beige color. Should be a step lighter than the light Reddish Brown, yet maintain a contrast with White.

Procedure:

1. Using medium brown, outline all areas, eyes, bags under the eyes, but NOT forehead wrinkles. Hold pattern under the face. Check lines in mirror.

2. White: fill in Area A.

3. Pale Beige: Areas B, C.

4. Light Red Brown: Areas D, E, F.

5. Medium Red Brown: Areas G, H.

6. No. 25 Red Brown: Areas J, K, L, M, N. Also shadowed dip in forehead.

7. No. 25 Brown: Line forehead wrinkles, shadow along mouth (along bottom of Area A) and top of Area G.

8. Pale Beige Highlight: Worry pouches above eyes between worry lines on forehead. Cheek bones.

9. Light Red Brown: Spots, freckles, muzzle (Areas A and B).

10. Black: Eyes, eye brow, side of nose, cheeks, mouth, chin, nose.

11. Red: Lips, a line below mouth-line.

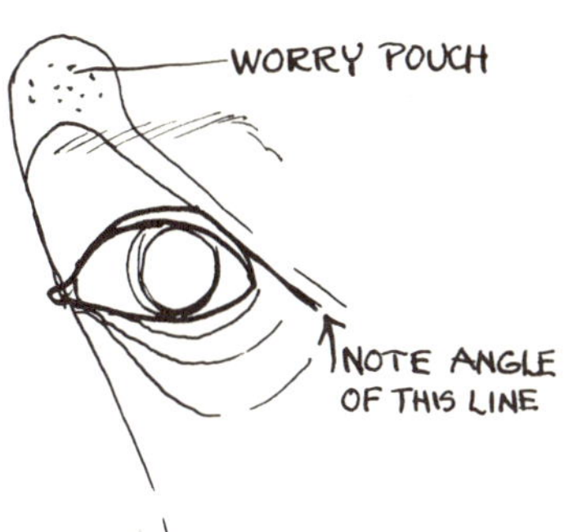

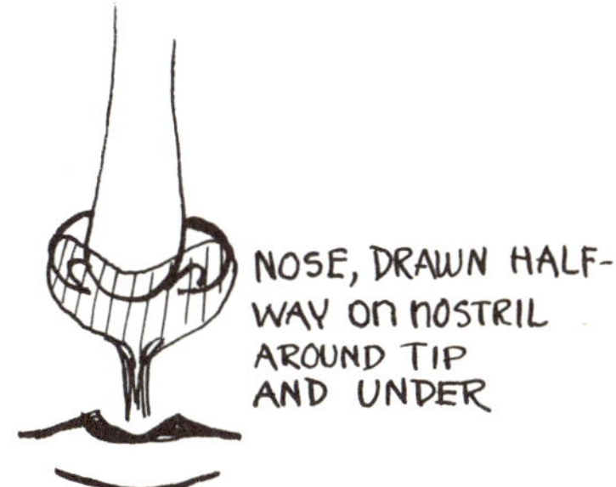

COSTUME FOR MR. SLOE, A TORTOISE

Materials:

T-shirt: grey-brown

Gym shorts: any color, with short legs

Slippers: house slippers of the slide type, or any soft shoe

Fabrics: brown jersey (or similar fabric which will drape well, such as cotton sheet blankets or rayon crepe), for head, arms, legs

heavy black canvas or ducking, for toes, straps, under-shell

cotton, grey-brown, for wimple

soft-green felt, for under-shell

Dacron, or cotton batting

½ inch elastic

Brown rubber floor mat (or rubber runner, sold by foot)

Jumbo hooks and eyes, or the large single hooks used on waist bands

Aluminum clothes line wire

hoop wire

Fiber glass resin

Fiber glass cloth

Fiber glass paint, soft green

Screen wire, or fine mesh chicken wire

Twill tape

Button thread

Masking tape

Flat black paint (Latex or Show Card)

Button thread

Desired Effect:

The giant tortoise navigates with an incredibly controlled, slow and dignified movement. These qualities are dominant in the character of Mr. Sloe. Once in the shell, the actor will begin to understand *why* he moves this way. The construction of feet and legs which gives the bulky and bow-legged look, will call for slow, well-placed steps. Neck movement is particularly characteristic of the tortoise and, as he slowly stretches it and moves his head, the folds under the chin will give an aged and weathered quality. In contrast to all the other animals, and particularly to the hare, he should appear as if caught by a slow-motion camera.

Basic Garments:

The actor will wear a t-shirt to which the turtle sleeves are affixed. This shirt could be short sleeved. Gym shorts will serve to fasten legs to, and should fit well at the waist. Sides of shorts may need to be covered with brown fabric if they are visible through cracks in sides of shell. The slipper slides will be sewed to the turtle foot.

Hands:

Shape aluminum wire into an oval which will encircle the hand with fingers spread, extending slightly beyond. Cut same shape from brown rubber floor matting, and whip to wire with button thread.

Draw pattern for toes, noting that large toe leans inward. Allow extra room for stuffing. Cut two from grey-brown cotton, and two from heavy canvas. Sew edges, trim, clip curves, and turn. Stuff each toe with dacron. Whip to wire on top side of sole. Sew an elastic band to go across hand, for control.

Feet:

Shape aluminum wire same as for hands, encircling the foot. The wire should be somewhat straight on the outside of the foot, flaring away from the foot on the inside. Cut this shape from rubber. Whip to wire. Sew a house slipper to the rubber sole to keep actor's foot in place. Any type soft shoe would serve this purpose. An elastic strap over the foot, attached to foot wire at the back sides, might aid control of foot.

Draw toe pattern around end of foot-wire. Note position of large toe. Prepare as for hands.

Arms:

Measure around hand wire. Cut a piece of jersey in that width, and twice the length of the arm. Run gathering threads down middle. Gather to fit from high up on shoulder to hand wire. On under side, sew a two inch band of cotton down gathering line to form a casing for hoop wire. Run hoop wire into casing, and secure to wire of hand and on t-shirt shoulder. Sew into tube shape.

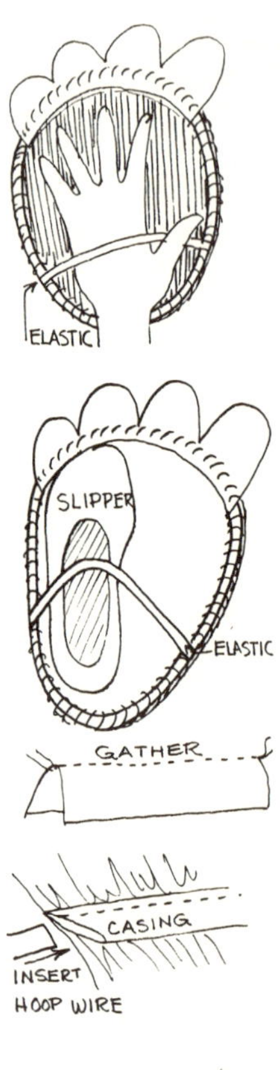

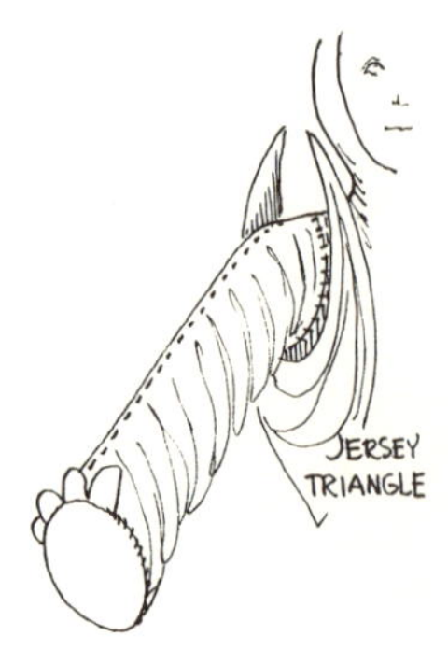

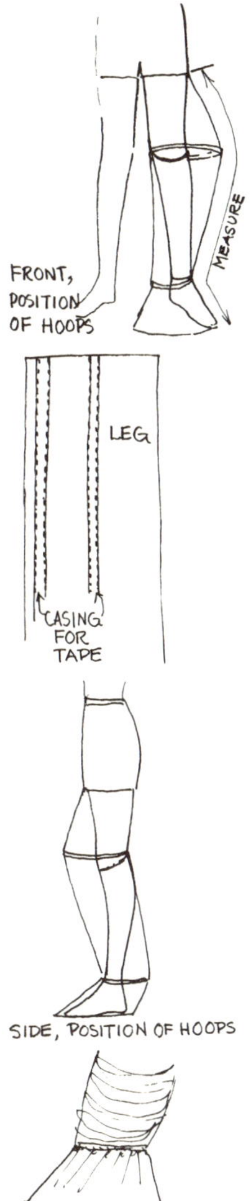

Sew end of Jersey tube to hand wire, and to t-shirt around the arm hole, pulling it up over the shoulder.

Cut a 24 inch square of jersey. Cut it diagonally into two triangles. Drape the triangle under the arm to form extra folds of "skin," lapping ends at top. Tack outside edges and ends.

Legs:

Proceed in same way as for arms. Make a circle of hoop wire, about 26 inches in circumference. Hold hoop against inside of knee, and allow circle to push to outside of leg. Overlap end of wire, and tape with masking tape.

Make an elastic garter which fits just below the knee. Fasten to hoop on inside of the leg, and at the back of the leg.

Make another hoop wire circle, holding it against the outside of the ankle. Have foot wire in place, and let the ankle hoop push to the inside of leg, but not as far to the inside as the foot wire. See relationship in design. Fasten wire with tape.

Make elastic garter to fit just above ankle. Fasten to ankle wire on outside of leg, and at front of leg.

Measure around all leg hoops. Cut jersey in the width of the largest hoop, and twice the length of the leg as measured from foot wire to bottom of shorts.

Next to the seam line on one side, and down the center, sew a one inch strip of jersey to form casing. Have all hoops on leg in proper position, and measure from bottom of shorts on outside of leg to floor. Do the same for the inside of leg. Cut twill tape to these measurements, run into casings, and gather. Gather top of jersey tube to fit around leg of shorts. Sew in place.

Slip tube over hoops, distributing gathers along leg and down to ankle. Leave smooth from ankle to floor. Tack through tube and twill tape where hoops meet at inside and outside of legs. Sew bottom of tube to foot wire. Ease in fullness at ankle wire, and whip jersey to wire.

Head:

Make a basic wimple from grey-brown
cotton. Put on actor, and with cotton or
dacron batting form the two humps on the
top and to the outside of the head. Cut a 24
inch square of jersey. Cut into 2 triangles.
Stretch jersey along forehead edge of wimple, over humps, pulling down and away
from the face, to the back. Tack to wimple.
Gather in excess at back. Pull other triangle
under chin, upward. Where jersey meets,
tuck under top piece. Arrange in folds under chin. Sew on right side; pin and mark
for hooks and eyes on left side. Folds under chin will need to be pulled slightly to
back to keep neck somewhat skinny. Round
off corner of jersey under neck.

Tortoise Shell:
Back:

Cut from screen wire or fine mesh chicken
wire the shell shape shown in diagram. Cut,
slit, overlap, and wire in shape. Adjust proportion to fit actor. Be sure the curved areas
in front and in back of the legs are cut out
enough to allow freedom of movement. It
will be somewhat constricting, but will work
if the actor keeps turtle movements slow.
Roll under outside edges of screen wire to
give dimension, and to eliminate snags.

Draw with chalk or magic marker the
hexagons f o u n d o n t h e tortoise s h e l l.
Squeeze and bend wire where identations
are desired. (Chicken wire does this best.)
Push up for humps. These need not be too
distinctly defined, as painting will complete
the illusion.

Fiber glass is the only material which will
be light, and yet strong enough for the shell.
It is tricky, but not impossible, for an ama-
teur to work with. However, consult your
local dealer for details concerning the process. Always work in a well ventilated room,
and avoid prolonged breathing of the fumes.
With your dealer's help, choose a heavy
weight fiber glass cloth. He may suggest
two layers. It is cut and handled like any
cloth.

Lay the fiber glass cloth over the wire
shell, pressing it into the indentations. Paint
the resin onto the cloth, smooth with the

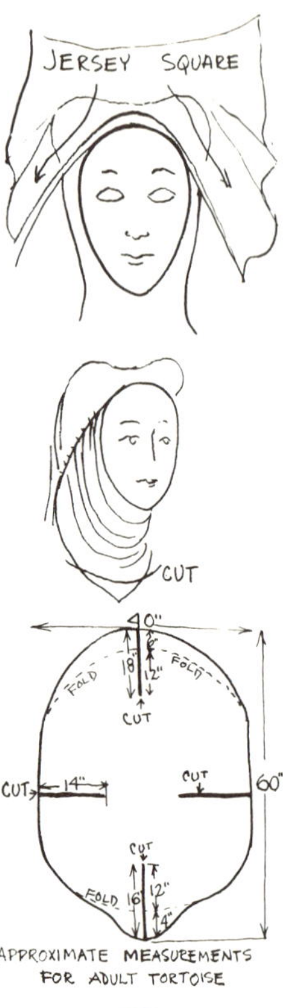

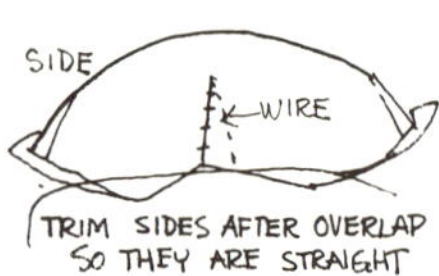

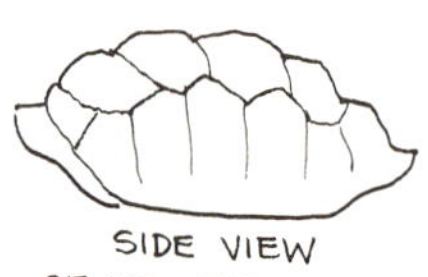

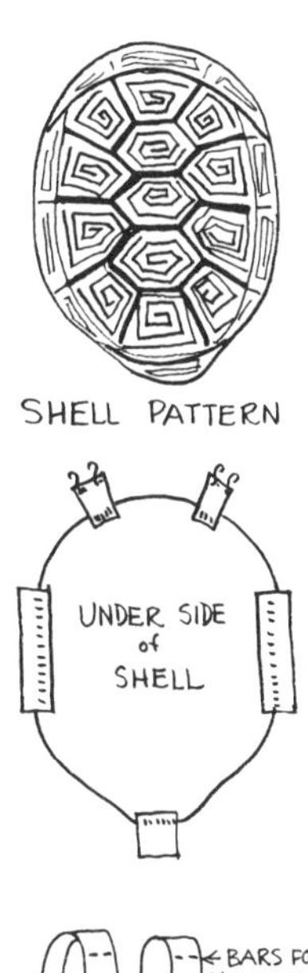
SHELL PATTERN

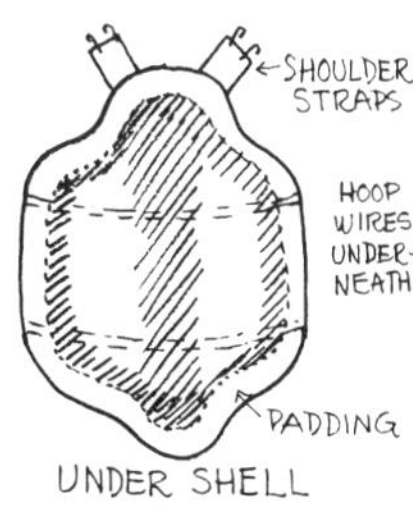

SHELL HARNESS

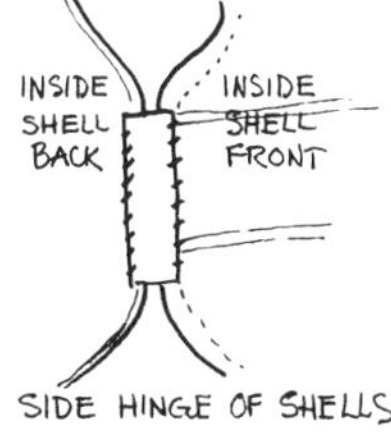

UNDER SHELL

SIDE HINGE OF SHELLS

brush as you go. Pay attention to the outside edges, cutting the fiber glass a little larger than the screen, so it can be stroked smoothly over the edges of the wire. Fiber glass will set exactly as you leave it, but it may be sandpapered for smoothness. Setting time depends on the climate, but it is fairly fast.

Paint with the special paint, recommended by the dealer, a soft green (or brown) as the base coat. Paint the line design in black.

Holes can be made in fiber glass with an ice pick, or hammer and nail. With button thread sew a strong strap of canvas to the sides for fastening to the front. Wide (4 or 5 inch) straps should go across the shoulders; and a hinge between the legs. The shoulder straps hook with heavy jumbo hooks onto bars sewed on shoulder of harness.

Harness:

Make a harness from canvas straps which go over shoulder to a band fastened securely around the waist. Sew pieces between straps, front and back, to keep them on shoulders.

Under-shell:

Cut pattern from cardboard. It should reach from collar bone of actor to about 4 inches above the knee at the center. It curves in under the arms and above the legs. Put on back shell, to see that the under-shell meets it along the sides. Let it bell out slightly in front.

Cut from soft-green felt lined with heavy canvas. Sew edges. Turn. Reach inside to edges, and lay a roll of dacron batting about 3 inches thick along the outer edge. Close opening. Top stitch next to roll. On under side (canvas side), whip two hoop wires into place, fastening them securely at ends. Sew canvas shoulder straps to top. They will hook to top of straps on back shell. Sew hinge from back shell to right side of under-shell. On the left side, the two shells will hook together with jumbo hooks. The hinge flap between the legs will hook to the under-shell. With any type black paint (poster, latex, or flat black), brush shadow along puffed rim on under-shell. Also down the center to suggest concavity.

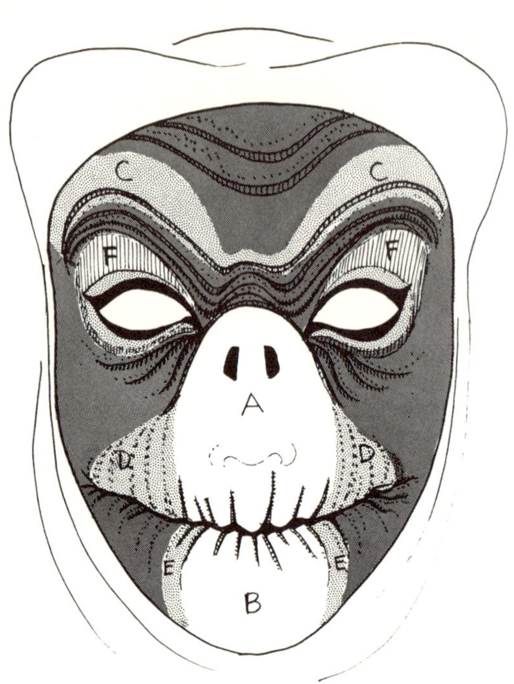

MR. SLOE, A TORTOISE

Make-Up Supplies

Stein's Grease Stick:
   No. 22 White

Stein's Grease Liner:
   No. 17 Black
   No. 7 Brown
   No. 25 Red-Brown
   No. 3 Moist Rouge

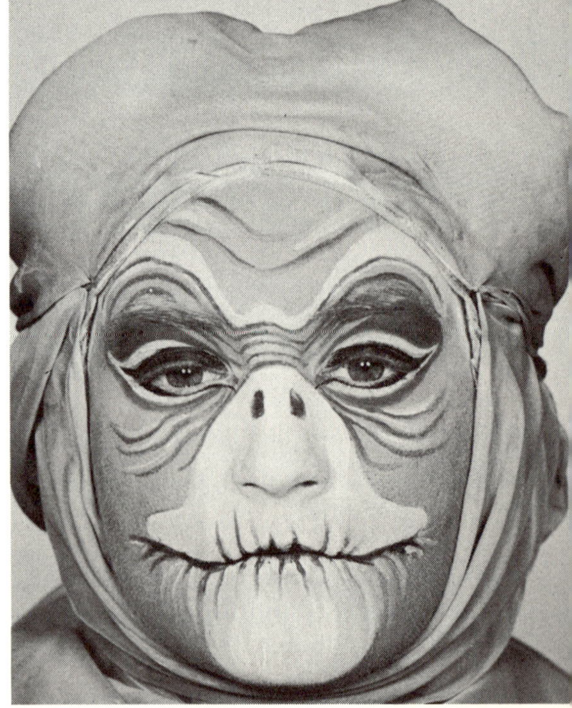

MAKE-UP FOR MR. SLOE, A TORTOISE

Mix	**Effect Desired**
1. No. 7 Brown Liner No. 22 White	Medium Brown.
2. Same colors as above with more white	Medium Tan, light enough to contrast with medium Brown and yet be dark against White highlight.

Procedure:

1. Using medium Brown outline major areas—mouth, eyes, eye-bags, eyelids and shadow above, but not the wrinkles.

2. White: Fill in Areas A and B.

3. Black: Fill in Turtle's eyes.

4. Tan: Create eyelids above eyes, and bags below. Fill in Areas C, D, E.

5. Medium Brown: Fill in rest of face except Area F above the eyes.

6. No. 25 Red-Brown: Fill in Area F above the eyes. Draw in all wrinkles.

7. White: Draw wrinkles from side of Turtle's nose (Area A) out to corner of Area D. Draw wrinkles from side of chin (Area B) out slightly beyond Area E.

8. Tan: Highlight between forehead wrinkles, above wrinkles, beneath eye, and at corners of mouth.

9. With Black: Draw in mouth line. Be sure "zig-zag" wrinkle effect is created on both upper and lower lips. Draw on nostrils. They will fall to either side of the bridge of the nose.

10. Add a touch of Red on the inner corners of eyes.

COSTUME FOR MR. FLEET, A HARE

Materials:

T-shirt: light grey

Tights: light grey

Two pair socks: one large man's size
one extra large man's size, with long tops

Slippers

Fabrics: light grey cotton, for wimple
white net, for tail and under-belly
pink organdy, for ears
white interfacing (Pellon), for ears

Rubber floor mat

12″ Maribou rope trim

Dacron batting

Millinery wire

Elastic

Desired Effect:

This boastful, cocky hare must seem slim, even bony and athletic.
In short, he must look as though he can carry out his arrogant claims
of fleetness. He is debonair in his light grey coat with white "tuxedo"
front and overstated tail. One ear at a rakish angle, his puckish face
poised for a flippant remark, large rear feet ready for takeoff, he main-
tains a prize fighter's stance of confident expectancy.

Basic Garments:

The t-shirt, tights, 2 pair extra large men's socks, and cotton for wimple, could be dyed light grey at the same time. Take the nylon tights out first, as they dye quickly. The t-shirt should be tight fitting.

Body:

To create a more thin, bony look, as befits a lithe racing creature, make knobs on elbows and at knees with dacron padding. Cover with patches of light grey cotton. Whip in place.

Draw the white patch on front of shirt. Cut same shape from two layers of white net, only make it wider at the top. Sew sides of net down and gather in at the top. Sew.

Tail:

Use white net, and follow instructions as given for Mrs. Warren, the rabbit.

Hands:

Use the dyed grey socks and follow the instructions given for Mrs. Warren, the rabbit.

Feet:

Start with a pair of Jiffy house slippers, or T.V. slippers. Place shoe on rubber rug runner. Draw pattern which will extend toes 4 inches and heel one inch. Cut soles ¼ inch wider than shoes. Use the grey-dyed long topped socks. Cut the foot in two. Estimate how much is needed from the top of sock to extend the toe to fit the rabbit sole pattern. Cut this piece off and sew as extension onto foot. Put elastic in top of sock.

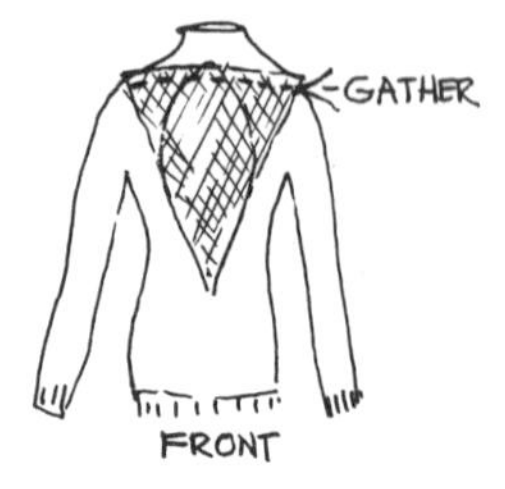

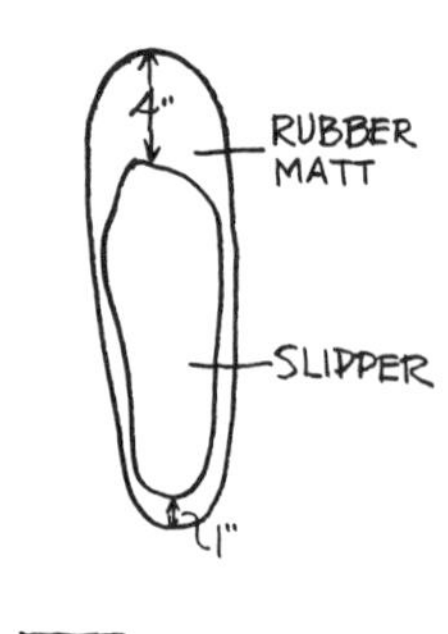

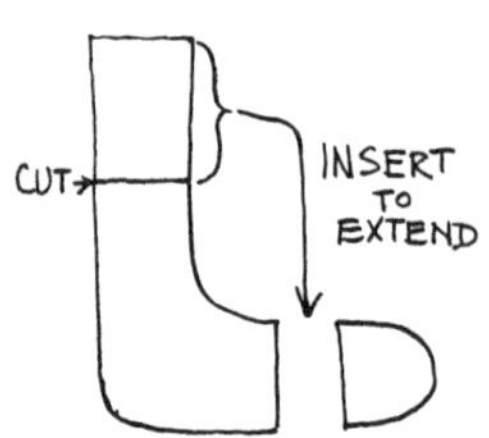

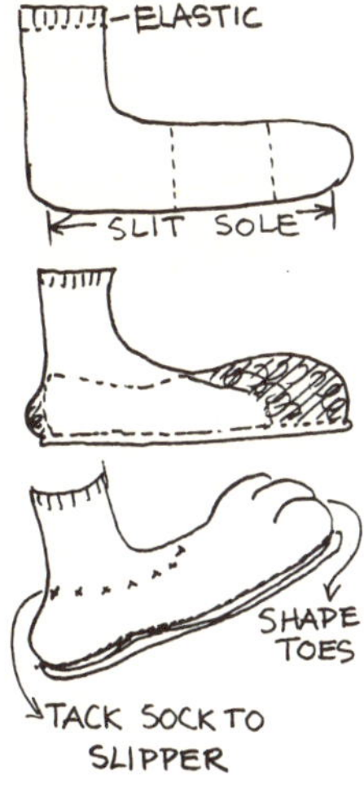

Make slit on center bottom of the sock, being cautious about cutting too far on heel and toe.

Shape paw with dacron padding over toe of shoe, and out over extended toe, making it higher at the end. Open the slit in the sole of sock and lay it over the padding. Put actor's foot in. Turn under extra sock on sides. Sew with button thread through the rubber sole. Mark toe lines, and sew down through padding with a large backstitch to shape the toes. Attach top of slipper to sock along sides and front. If possible, sew some portion of the edge of the sole of the inner slipper to the rubber sole beneath.

Head:

Cut basic wimple of light grey cotton. Take darts on sides to make a skinny, fitted neck. Sew loop of maribou by edge of cheek. See design for placement: the bottom comes opposite the mouth.

Ears:

Cut two ears from a layer of pale pink organdy, grey cotton, and white pellon interfacing. Sew three thicknesses together. Turn. Top stitch 1/4 inch from edge, and gather bottom. Run millinery wires up sides. Fold, ears at bottom, with opening forward, and pink to the inside. Lay against the head, behind the maribou. Tack to wimple. Bend one ear forward.

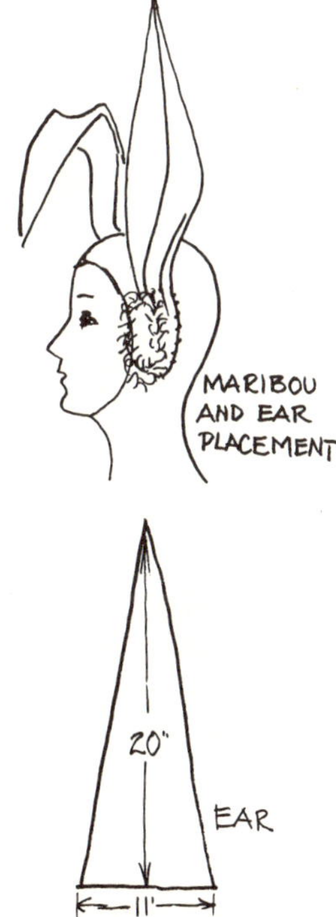

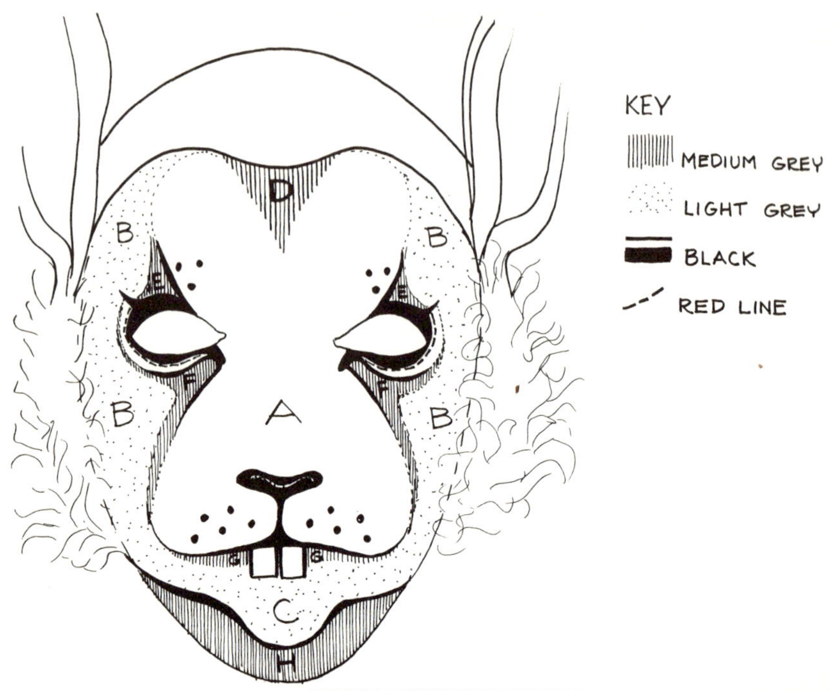

MR. FLEET, A HARE

Make-Up Supplies

Stein's Grease Stick:
 No. 22 White

Stein's Liner Stick:
 No. 17 Black

Moist Rouge:
 No. 3 Medium Red

Liquid Black tooth wax

Alcohol: to remove wax

MAKE-UP FOR MR. FLEET, A HARE

Mix	Effect Desired
1. No. 22 White No. 25 Black	Light Grey
2. Same colors as above	Medium Grey
3. No. 22 White No. 3 Moist Rouge	Dark Pink

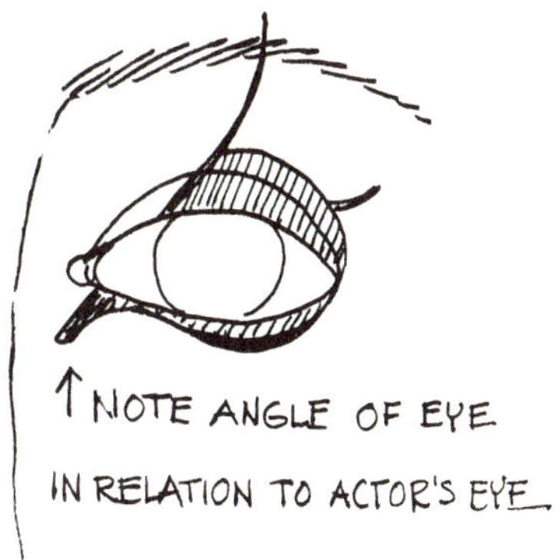

Procedure:

1. Medium Grey: Outline all areas and lines.

2. White: Area A and teeth. Bags under eyes.

3. Light Grey: Areas B, C.

4. Medium Grey: Areas D, E, F, G, H.

5. Black: Pupils, lines above and below eyes, chops, teeth, chin.

6. Red: Along black pupils above white bag under eyes. Inner corner of eye.

7. For best effect of teeth, black out teeth with liquid black tooth wax.

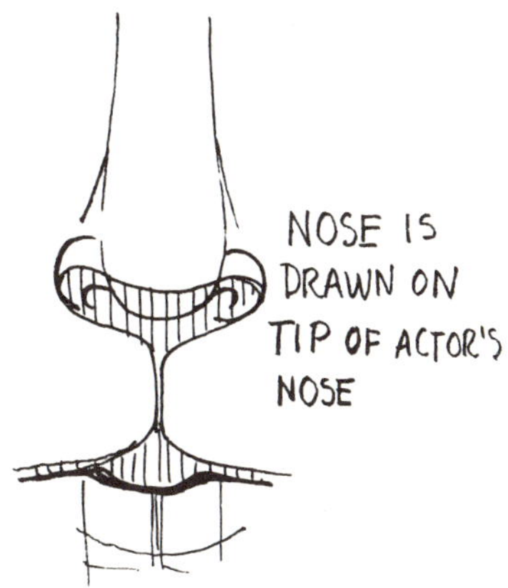

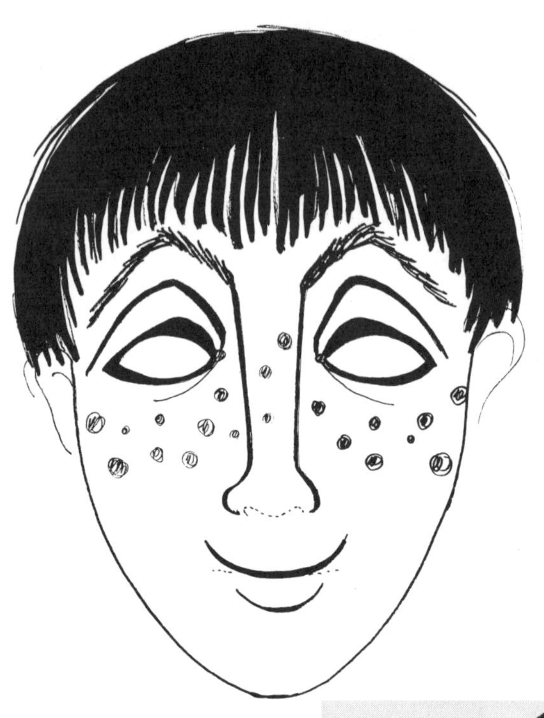

GEORGE

Make-Up Supplies:

Base:
  No. 7, Light Sunburn

Laying in color:
  No. 25 Brown

Lines and Freckles:
  No. 17 Black

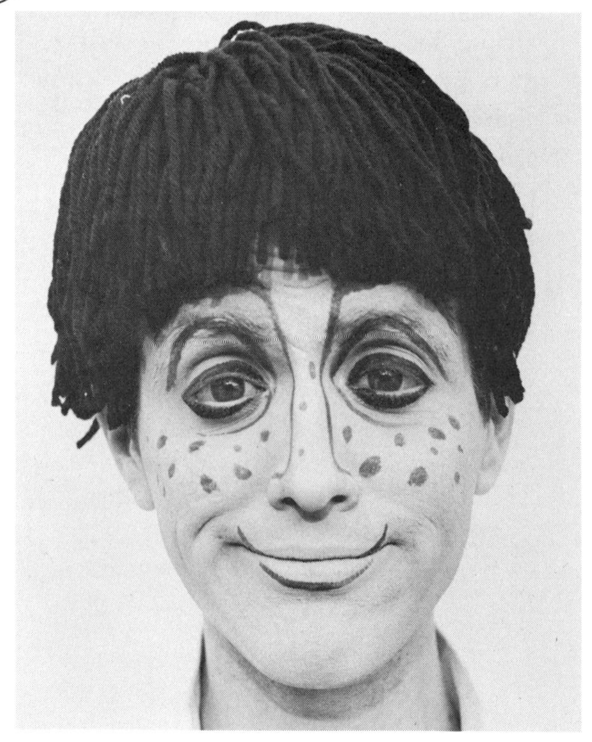

Make-up:

The people-make-up is styled to complement the animals, with painted features and yarn hair. Their movement should be puppet-like, with exaggerated mime. This stylization combined with the gobble-de-gook speech, or even the total elimination of speech by people, will set them apart from the animal world. This movement might be styled after the mechanical maneuvers of a tightly-wound doll; or after the rapid, stick-like gyrations of an early Charlie Chaplin movie.

Make-up Procedure:

After removing cold cream, soap eyebrows by wetting a bar of soap and rubbing it on brows until all hairs lie flat. Allow to dry. Apply base, being certain eyebrows and lips are covered. Use a brown tone, and lightly sketch in all feature lines which are indicated in the design as heavy black lines. The outline around the eyes, is thick enough, in all cases, that it covers the natural eyelid. Then the new eyelid is drawn above that; and the new eyebrow above that. If heavy lines are indicated down the sides of the nose, and around the nostrils, they are to be drawn exactly like that, onto the face. When no heavy lines are shown for nose or mouth, they are to be left plain, except for base covering. Lips are located in relation to the natural lip, but do not follow the natural lip line: do it as it is shown. The opening of the drawn lip will always correspond with the natural opening. Eyelashes are painted onto the face. (If, in addition to the painted eyelashes, you wish to experiment with gluing long lashes cut from organdy, this would be in keeping with the style. Regular false eyelashes would be lost.) After establishing all lines, paint them on in pure black grease.

Rouge is applied in round circles of color. The lips of Mrs. Urban-Notcouth can be outlined with black. The tiny smile line on Jackie and Robin can be done in a tiny black line. Sophia deliberately has that pale, all-eye look.

The author has made sufficient in-
dication concerning costuming.
Choose the contemporary garment
which will most obviously reveal the
character stereotype.

Just as the animal fur, or hair, is
translated into fabrics which repre-
sent reality; in executing the people
it is necessary to re-interpret their
hair into a more styled form. For
this reason, yarn wigs are recommended.

To make the base, or skull cap for
the wig, pin several layers of nylon
net together, around the shape of
the head, as in making a wimple. Be
sure hair line is covered, and cut
away into a curve behind the ears.
It should fit snugly, and have elastic
along the bottom, in the back.

Sew heavy cotton or synthetic rug
yarn to skull cap in layers, working
in rows from top to bottom. Trim,
and pull into desired shape. To hold
the yarn threads in position, arrange
them, and then sew through center
of threads in long, loose stitches. For
a pouf effect, such as Mrs. Urban-
Notcouth, and Brando, make the
shape first in dacron batting. Cover
with cotton fabric to match hair,
then sew on yarn. Try using the
top of a nylon hose for the bald pate
of Mr. Urban-Notcouth. The hair
will have to cover the point where
the stocking is sewed up to form the
cap.

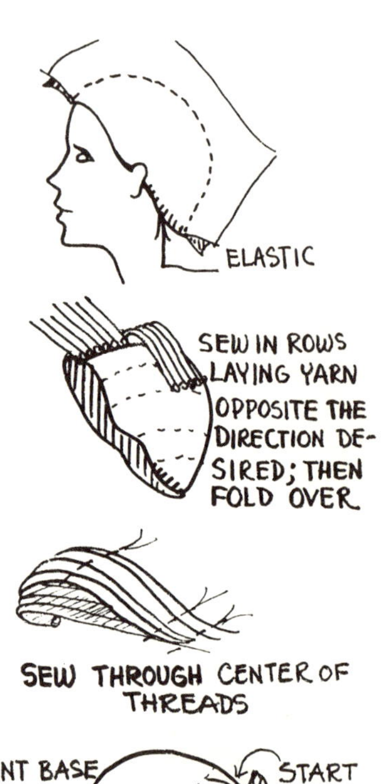

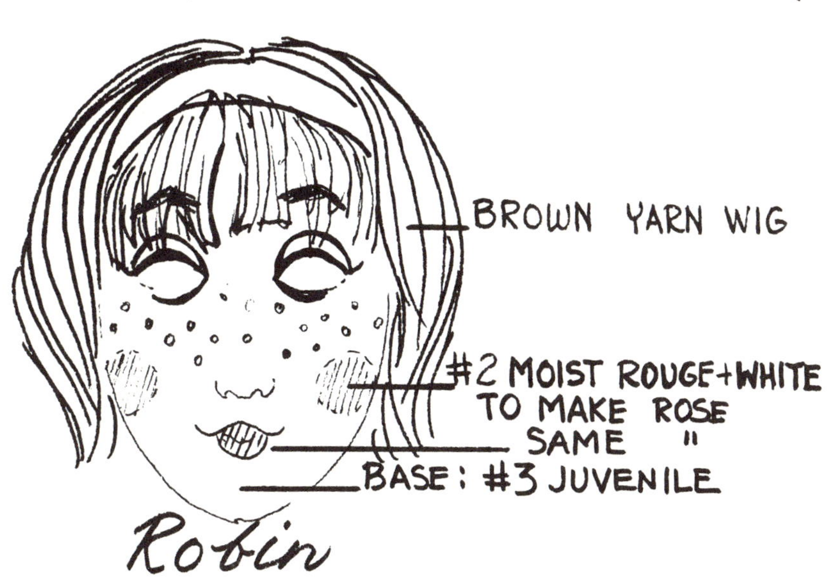

YELLOW YARN WIG
BASE: #3 JUVENILE
#2 MOIST ROUGE PLUS
WHITE TO MAKE ROSE
SAME AS ABOVE
Jackie
BROWN YARN WIG
#2 MOIST ROUGE+WHITE
TO MAKE ROSE
SAME "
BASE: #3 JUVENILE
Robin

RED YARN WIG ROLLED OVER EXTRA LARGE ROLLERS
#2 PALE JUVENILE
Sophia

BLACK YARN WIG
BASE: #11 SALLOW
Brando

Mr. Urban-Notcouth

Mrs. Urban-Notcouth

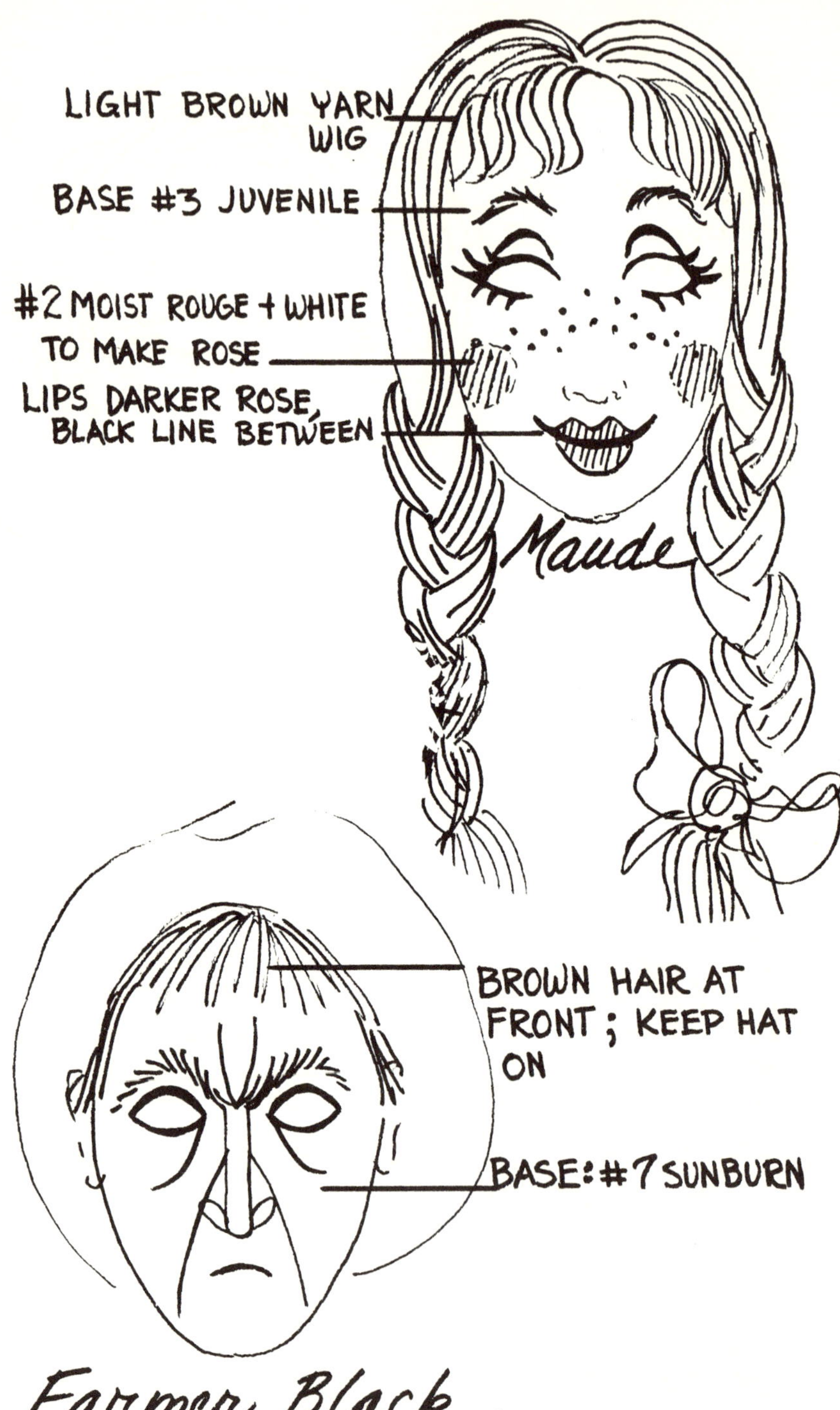

LIGHT BROWN YARN WIG
BASE #3 JUVENILE
#2 MOIST ROUGE + WHITE TO MAKE ROSE
LIPS DARKER ROSE, BLACK LINE BETWEEN
Maude
BROWN HAIR AT FRONT; KEEP HAT ON
BASE: #7 SUNBURN
Farmer Black

Mrs. Stainer

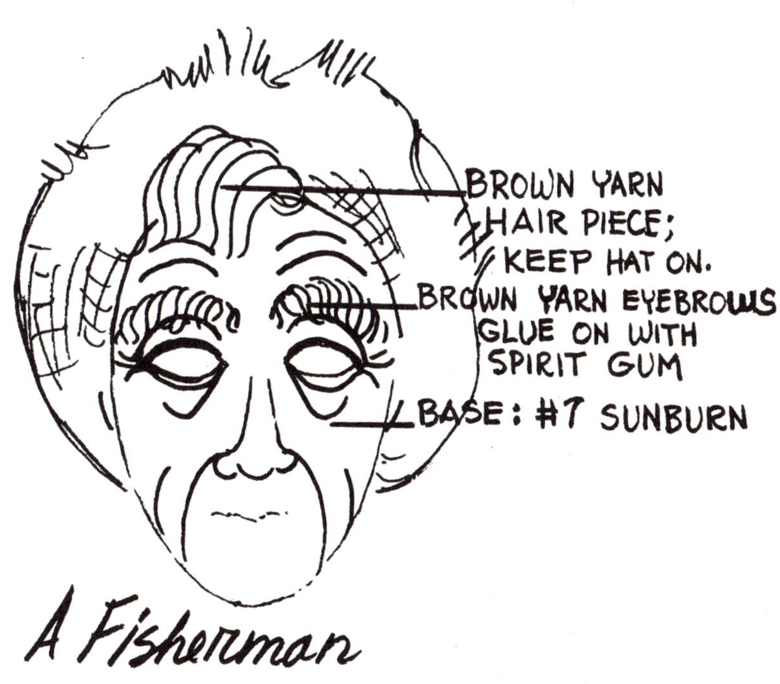

A Fisherman

STAGING

The author has set forward simple and highly workable plans for staging this play. As another point of departure, the following suggestions concerning staging for *THE GREAT CROSS COUNTRY RACE* are made. The dimensions included are for a hypothetical situation and should be re-evaluated in terms of the producer's local stage. To seek to offset the spasmodic opening and closing of the curtains, which tends to make the play episodic, a scheme is needed that allows the action to flow continually before the audience, giving a sense of unity. It will also eliminate problems of properly lighting the characters running up and down the aisles of a darkened theatre.

Set Design:

One solution is to create a screen unit, framed by trees, on which moving scenery is projected from the back side. When the sense of moving from one place to another is required, the running takes place in front of the screen, with the forest moving in the opposite direction, stopping at the projection of the next scene. Set pieces should be kept simple, and highly stylized, so that the scenery is relatively neutral.

Transitions between scenes are accomplished by having the actors walk past the moving scenery, exiting just as the character for the new scene enters, in front of the projection showing the new locale. Some continuity scenes should be kept in for the sake of character development, while others not necessary for covering scene changes can be eliminated.

Transition Plan:

A suggested plan for transitions is the following:

ACT I

Scene 1: The Badger exits yawning, as the scenery begins to revolve behind him, stopping on the bramble thicket projection.

Scene 2: The Tortoise exits, with the scenery moving behind him, as the fisherman enters with picnic basket. The scene stops at the river bank as he settles down and goes to sleep. The Hare enters for the beginning of Scene 3.

Scene 3: The fisherman lies back, holding the pole with his knees, and is partially hidden by the bramble patch, so that the scene proceeds without his being noticed. As the scene changes to grassy bank, the Hedgehog crosses, carrying the large arrow sign.

Scene 4: The scene changes back to the river bank behind the girl's entrance. The Fisherman sits up as his bell rings.

Scene 7: Instead of sitting, the couple exits, holding hands. Continuity scene 7 takes place in front of moving scenery, ending with cornfield projection.

Scene 8: Run continuity scene 8 in front of scenery as it moves to the cottage.

Scene 9: In the cottage garden, behind the rock wall, Mrs. Stainer sets up the clothes line pole, the other one being anchored offstage. At the end, she gathers dirty clothes and the pole and stomps off.

Scene 10: The scenery moves behind the animals as they gather again at the rock quarry. The race is carried on as if it is lapping around the stage, with the runners exiting one side, and entering from the opposite side.

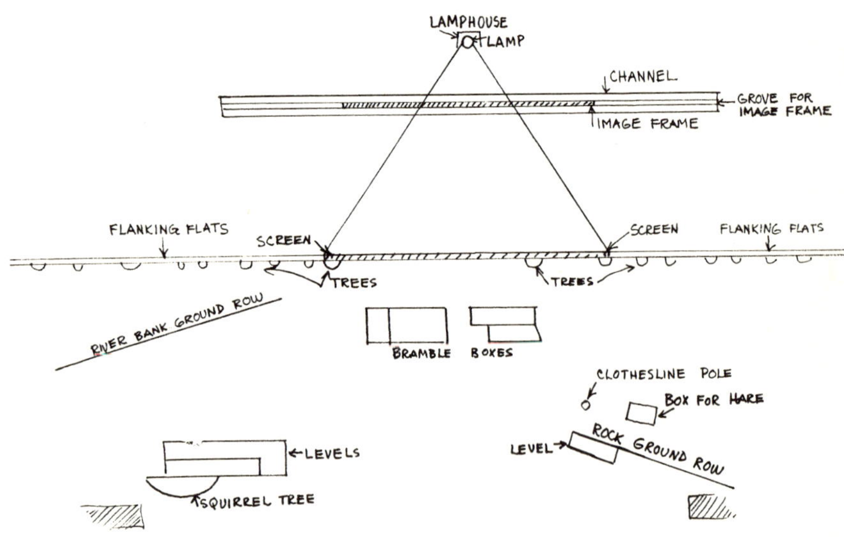

LAMPHOUSE
LAMP
CHANNEL
GROVE FOR
IMAGE FRAME
IMAGE FRAME
FLANKING FLATS
SCREEN
SCREEN
FLANKING FLATS
TREES
TREES
RIVER BANK GROUND ROW
BRAMBLE BOXES
CLOTHESLINE POLE
BOX FOR HARE
LEVELS
ROCK GROUND ROW
LEVEL
SQUIRREL TREE

Style of Set:

In keeping with the stylization of the humans and animals in this play, the same quality is carried into the scenery by using screen wire to achieve the sharp, crisp lines of paper sculpture. The wire will keep its shape in large pieces, will bend on the straight or curved lines, and will bell out to give rounded dimension. It can be brushed or spray painted. Bend the cut edges under, so costumes will not catch on the sharp wires.

Colors:

Both the projected sky and the sky behind the trees on the regular flats are blue. All screen - wire foliage is green. The flat tree trunks, cut from beaver board, are painted a light, warm brown. Because the projected tree trunks will be white, unity can be maintained by painting the screen wire trunks eggshell white with accent lines in black. Hills, rock details, weeds on the river bank, etc., would also be in black lines. Rocks, and the rock wall should be yellow ochre with a touch of burnt sienna. The river bank ground row, and bramble mound, can be mossy green. In all cases, the paint used should have a flat finish.

Instead of painting flats and ground rows, they can be covered with inexpensive colored cotton fabric. Burlap is particularly good under lights.

SET PIECES: (All basic units are on stage at all times.)

Trees. The squirrel's tree has a projecting limb at such a height that the animals who stand behind on the levels, can peer over at the lovers. Cut trunk and branches from beaver board, or ¼″ plywood, and reinforce with wood on back. Cut the foliage shape from screen wire; also a piece the shape of the trunk, only wider so that it will bell out in the center when fastened on the sides. Give dimension to the side limb in the same way. Cut a triangular shape for the burl from screen. Wire onto trunk so that it forms a protrusion.

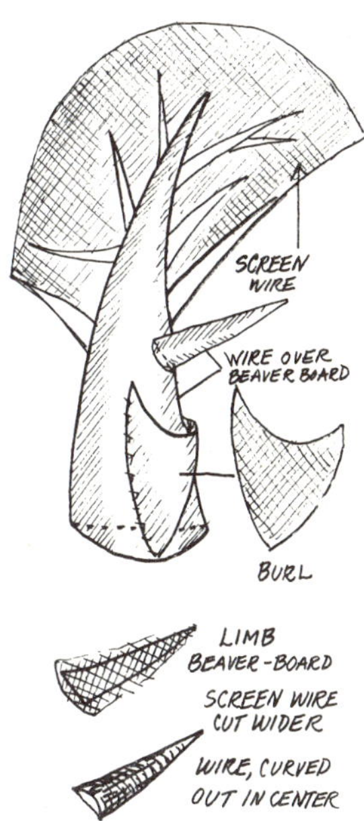

Use the same process for all trees, applying screen wire forms to trunks of those on the projection screen and the regular flats.

River Bank Ground Row:

It is located behind the squirrel's tree, in such a position that the fisherman, leaning against the end of the bramble mound, can cast his line behind it.

Bramble Bush:

It is located at center stage, in front of the projection screen Make two solid box shapes, which are fastened to the floor. Face the front of the opening between the two boxes with bramble shapes made from double thicknesses of black pellon or heavy canvas which has a rib of hoop wire running between stitched casings. Attach thorn shapes, also stiffened with hoop wire. Thorns from one side will overlap those on the other side. The hare finally manages to back up between the thorns, with his head facing the audience.

The Rock Wall:

This ground row serves for the Urban-Notcouth scene, and for Mrs. Stainer's garden. She brings the clothes line pole to the inside corner of the wall, with the line attached offstage. A level should be behind the wall, under the line, where the Hare is actually standing when he **appears** to be hanging from the line. The line should be high enough to make him look really stretched. Slightly indicate rocks with black paint.

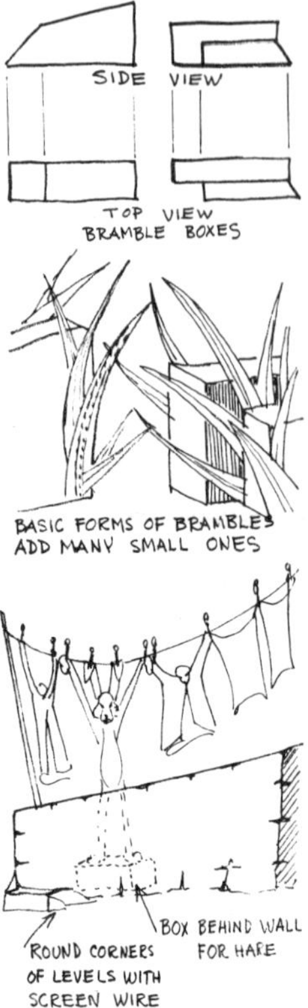

Projection Screen:

The projection screen backs the central stage area, a little to stage left. Cutout trees disguise its rectangular shape, and regular flats flank it on either side, with a continuation of sculptured trees. Lower the height of the flanking flats to 7′ or 8′, and make the trees closer together to suggest a dense woods. The projection screen, and the flanking flats are covered with a high grade cotton dress fabric, such as Bates disciplined cotton, or Fruit-O-The-Loom Pampered cotton. The fabric should have a matt surface, sheer enough to permit the light to saturate the fibers, yet thick enough to stop the light from passing on through. The color of the fabric should be a pastel shade of blue. Both screen and flats are flooded with soft blue light from the overhead borders. If space permits, the same effect can be achieved by placing blue floods behind ground rows.

In preparing both the screen and flanking flats, first sew the panels of cotton together. With the seams going up and down, stretch over the structure, pulling edges to the back side, and then staple. Do not use glue.

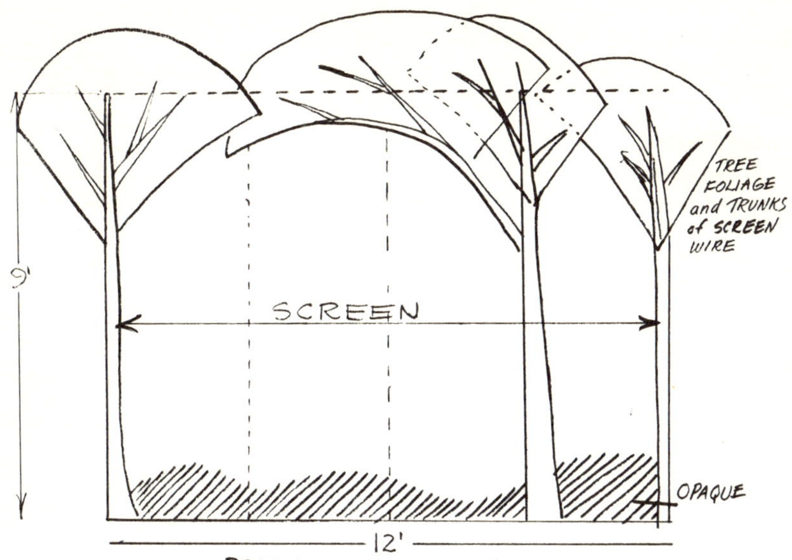

9'
SCREEN
TREE FOLIAGE and TRUNKS of SCREEN WIRE
OPAQUE
12'
PROJECTION SCREEN, FRONT

9'
SCREEN
CORNER BRACES FOLLOW BRANCHES OF TREES
FLANKING FLATS JOIN SCREEN ON SIDES
SOLID AREA BEAVER BOARD or PLYWOOD
3'
9'
PROJECTION SCREEN, BACK

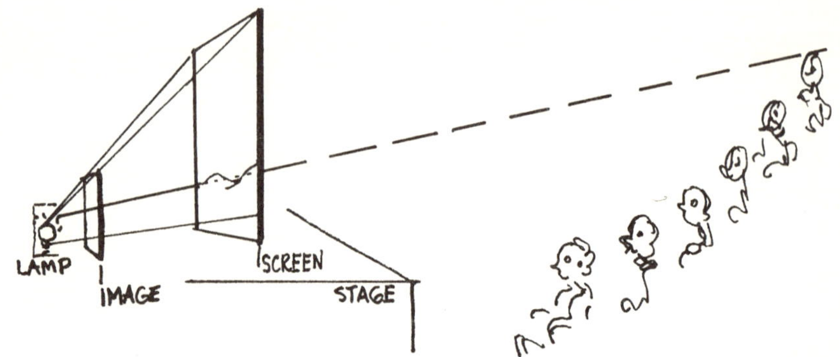

The lower "hill" area must be opaque (beaver board or plywood) so that the projection lamp is not seen by the audience. Determine the height of these hills by first placing the screen and projector in their proper place, and then sighting from the highest point at the rear of the theatre.

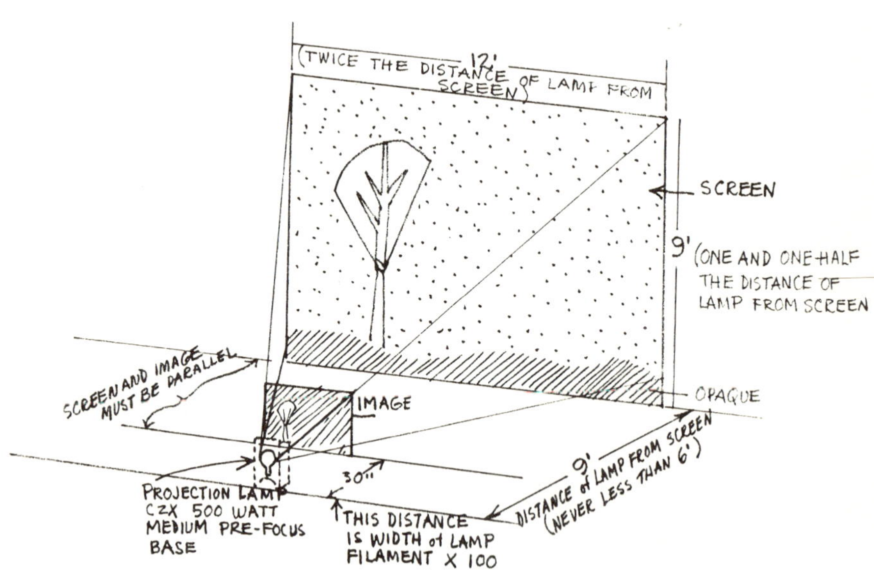

SET LIGHTING: Only soft general area light should fall upon the face of the screen. Light the areas of the action, such as the squirrel tree, etc., by spotlights. Overhead borders or floor floods light the forest flats and projection screen.

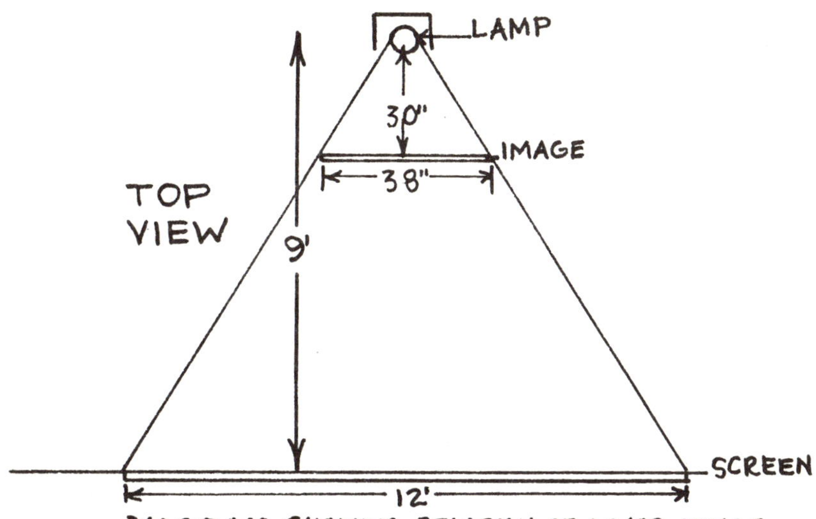

DIAGRAM SHOWING RELATION OF LAMP, IMAGE, AND SCREEN WHEN THE LAMP IS PLACED 9' FROM THE SCREEN

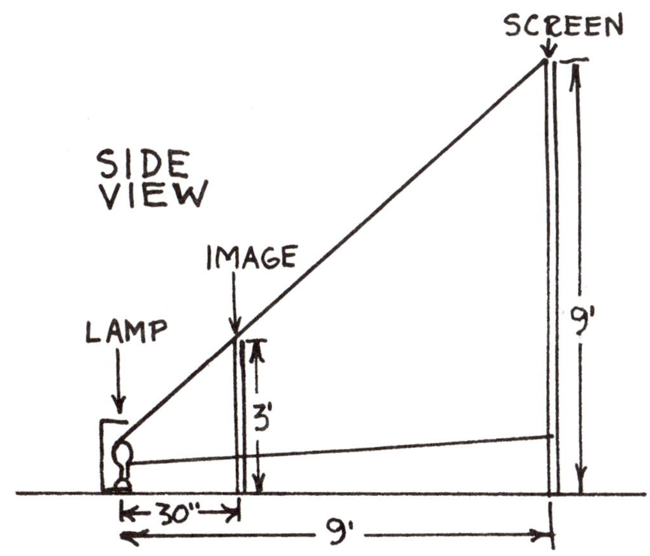

The Moving Scenery:

The moving scenery takes the form of patterns of light in the shape of trees, etc., projected upon the screen from the rear. These patterns are made by cutouts in heavy Kraft wrapping paper (60 or 70 lb.) or poster board which is attached to frames set in front of a projection lamp with a compact filament. The light passing through the holes falls upon the cloth screen. Colored transparent gelatines can be taped over these cutouts. Keeping the image frame **parallel to** the cloth screen eliminates distortion. Maintaining the proper distance between the filament of the projection lamp and the image frame provides clarity to the cut-out shapes.

Perspective Diagram

Generally speaking, the width of the screen should not exceed twice the distance of the lamp from the screen, nor the height more than 1½ times the distance of the lamp from the screen. The distance of the image frame from the lamp should not be less than 100 times the width of the filament. In the case of the CZX 500 watt projection lamp, with a filament approximately 5/16" square, the distance of lamp to image is about 30". Such a lamp may be purchased in a photo supply store. The base of this lamp is the medium prefocus type. A temporary lamphouse can be made with a standard 6" Fresnel spotlight, by removing *both* the lens *and* the reflector. For specialized equipment and further technical data, write the Hub Electric Co., 2255 West Grand Avenue, Chicago 60612, requesting free bulletin No. 107 —*Little Theatres from Modest Spaces*, or refer to the October 1962 issue of *Recreation Magazine* (National Recreation Association), "Scenery by Projection," p. 396 ff.

If the distance of the lamp from the screen is 6 feet, the maximum projection area will be about 9 by 12 feet, with an image frame size of approximately 5' wide and 4'6" high. However, if backstage space permits, the lamp can be moved back to 9' from the screen, leaving the projection area as it is, the image will be reduced to about 38" wide by 3" high, and the projection will be of a more even intensity overall. These are the measurements illustrated in the diagram.

Image Frames:

For the moving scenery, the image frame will be widened, at least twice, and preferably three times the width of a single image. The frame can be slid along the floor in a deep channel. Experiment to see the proportion of cutout scenery needed for projection. Be sure the cutouts clear the opaque section at the bottom of the screen.

To change image frames, slowly dim the projection lamp toward the end of the scene; replace the frame; raise lamp again. The end of one scene could be repeated on the beginning of the next frame for continuity.

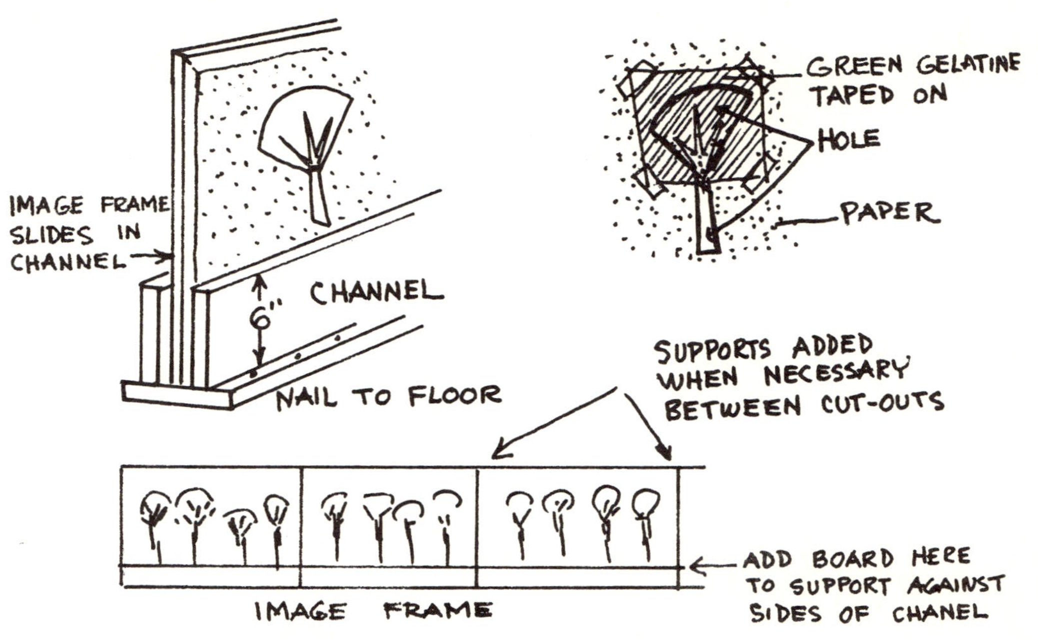

IMAGE FRAME SLIDES IN CHANNEL
CHANNEL
6"
NAIL TO FLOOR
GREEN GELATINE TAPED ON
HOLE
PAPER
SUPPORTS ADDED WHEN NECESSARY BETWEEN CUT-OUTS
ADD BOARD HERE TO SUPPORT AGAINST SIDES OF CHANEL
IMAGE FRAME